GATT Plus—A Proposal
for Trade Reform

Atlantic Council of the United States

Published for the
Atlantic Council of
The United States

The Praeger Special Studies program —
utilizing the most modern and efficient book
production techniques and a selective
worldwide distribution network — makes
available to the academic, government, and
business communities significant, timely
research in U.S. and international economic, social, and political development.

GATT Plus—A Proposal for Trade Reform

With the Text of the General Agreement

Report of the
Special Advisory Panel to the
Trade Committee of the
Atlantic Council

PRAEGER SPECIAL STUDIES IN INTERNATIONAL BUSINESS, FINANCE, AND TRADE

Praeger Publishers   New York   Washington   London

Library of Congress Cataloging in Publication Data

Atlantic Council of the United States.
  GATT plus—a proposal for trade reform

  (Praeger special studies in international business,
finance, and trade)
    1. Foreign trade regulation.   I. Contracting
Parties to the General Agreement on Tariffs and Trade.
General agreement on tariffs and trade. 1976. II. Title.
Law   341.7'54   76-126
ISBN 0-275-23010-4

PRAEGER PUBLISHERS
111 Fourth Avenue, New York, N.Y. 10003, U.S.A.

Published in the United States of America in 1975
by Praeger Publishers, Inc.

Printed in the United States of America

FOREWORD

I have always imagined that the phoenix emerged from the ashes arrayed in its brilliant plumage. The GATT which emerged from the ashes of the Havana Charter for an International Trade Organization was a modest institution. But it embodied the results of the largest multilateral trade negotiation in history accompanied by a code of trade rules designed to protect the tariff concessions from nullification or impairment by other restrictive measures and to establish the rule of non-discrimination in world trade. For over twenty years the General Agreement served as the basis for the trading relations of the principal trading nations. Apart from providing an effective forum for the settlement of trade disputes it organized a series of multilateral tariff conferences which steadily eroded tariff barriers to trade, culminating in the historic Kennedy Round which reduced the level of industrial tariffs across the board by some 35 percent whilst at the same time achieving some modest success in liberalizing some areas of agricultural trade. Through its provisions on customs unions and free-trade areas it successfully integrated the European Community and the European Free-Trade Association into the international trading system.

But like all human institutions it has inherent weaknesses (not the least of which is the problem of enforcement of the trade rules): it has had comparatively little success in dealing with the intractable problems of trade in agricultural products, trade in primary products, and in finding and providing an acceptable framework for dealing with the special trading problems of the developing countries. This latter failing led to the formation of UNCTAD (United Nations Conference on Trade and Development), which served the purpose of providing the developing countries with a political forum to focus world attention on their problems. The developing countries did not, however, forsake the GATT perhaps because they were inwardly conscious that they were beneficiaries to a considerable degree of the expansion of world trade, in which GATT has played so large a role, without themselves assuming any corresponding obligations.

The proliferation of less developed country participation in GATT (as well as that of a number of countries with state controlled economies) has, however, created problems which raise doubts as to the credibility of GATT and its development as an even more effective instrument for the orderly conduct of international trading relations. With certain exceptions decisions in GATT are taken by simple majority vote and it has become increasingly obvious that countries which accept legally binding and serious obligations governing their mutual trade would not indefinitely submit to a situation in which the administration of the trade rules would be governed by a body in which a vast majority of the members (and an increasingly organized majority), whilst enjoying all the benefits of the Agreement, has no equivalent commitments and yet by force of numbers has effective control of the decision-making process.

The Multilateral Trade Negotiations recently initiated in Geneva provide the opportunity for a long-needed revision and reinforcement and the Atlantic Council's Report, *GATT Plus: A Proposal for Trade Reform* provides to my mind an invaluable and constructive contribution to this task.

The report makes it clear beyond doubt that it is proposing no revision which would in any way discriminate against the developing countries; on the contrary they will benefit through the most-favored-nation clause from the increased liberalization of trade and the greater effectiveness of the code of liberalization. Moreover, as individual developing countries' economies develop, it will always be open for them to subscribe to the code and participate in its administration.

The introduction of weighted voting in the administration of the code is calculated to lend greater credibility to the organization's decision-making power and to encourage the acceptance of tighter obligations whose enforcement will take account of the weight of interests involved.

I heartily commend this report to the attention of the negotiators in the Multilateral Trade Negotiations which will shape the framework of international trade policy for the decades to come.

SIR ERIC WYNDHAM-WHITE
Former Director-General to GATT

PREFACE

GATT Plus: A Proposal for Trade Reform is the culmination of more than two years of study within the Atlantic Council. In February 1973 the Trade Committee of the Council called for action directed to the substantial liberalization of world trade as well as a reexamination of the adequacy of existing international institutions dealing with trade problems. It noted the need for more vigorous measures to reduce tariffs and other trade barriers and curb discriminatory and trade-distorting practices. It stated that while . . . "the General Agreement on Tariffs and Trade (GATT) has performed an essential role, consideration needs to be given to the adequacy of its procedures and mandate, which go back to the early post-war period, and to providing for a closer and more effective relationship between GATT and the International Monetary Fund."

The Trade Committee established a Special Advisory Panel to prepare detailed recommendations to implement these ideas. The Panel issued two interim reports. The first, released to the press on February 11, 1974, presented a preliminary sketch of a possible Code of Trade Liberalization among industrial nations supplementary to, and supportive of, GATT. The second report, published on March 26, 1974, proposed measures to strengthen the authority of the International Monetary Fund over trade measures applied for balance-of-payments purposes.

Since these reports were issued the Congress has enacted the Trade Act of 1974 and the Multilateral Trade Negotiations at Geneva have entered their initial stage. The present study, which elaborates and explains in detail the ideas sketched in the earlier interim reports, is therefore timely.

International trade fosters the exchange among nations not only of goods but also of services, technology and, of course, money. It is the stuff of economic interdependence and the vehicle through which the domestic economic conditions of one country influence those of others. Issues of trade policy are accordingly closely interwoven with domestic economic policies—so much so that, in economics, "domestic" and "foreign" are words whose significance diminishes almost daily. This is particularly true of the industrial nations whose trade with each other through an increasingly open system has rapidly mounted with the growing complexity of their economies as well as with gross national products. The trade between Western Europe, North America and Japan accounts for much the larger part of total world trade.

So it is the industrial nations which must set the pace for the continuing liberalization of world trade and for undertaking the improvements in international institutional arrangements required both to maintain the momentum of trade liberalization and to assure an effective means for enforcing trade rules and settling trade disputes in the years ahead. It is the purpose of *GATT Plus: A Proposal for Trade Reform* to contribute to public and official discussion of how these objectives may best be achieved as one of the possible results of the Multilateral Trade Negotiations just begun.

The Atlantic Council wishes to thank the members of the Special Advisory Panel (listed on page xi) who have served as joint rapporteurs for the report. The Panel has benefited from the comments and advice of members of the Trade Committee, especially its Chairman Lawrence C. McQuade. The members of the Trade Committee are listed on the inside back cover of the report. In addition, numerous individuals, government officials, international staff and others have made useful comments and criticisms. Panel members acknowledge, with special thanks, the suggestions of Miriam Camps, Virginia McClung, Albert Gerstein, John Jackson (author of *World Trade and the Law of GATT*), Margaret Potter, Anthony Solomon, and Sir Eric Wyndham-White, former Director-General of GATT, who has written the Foreword.

GATT Plus: A Proposal for Trade Reform is a collective document. While members of the Special Advisory Panel take sole responsibility for its contents, the Atlantic Council takes pleasure in presenting it for public discussion.

GATT Plus was originally published as a *Policy Paper* in the Atlantic Council's Trade Series. It is hoped that its appearance in the permanent, hardbound Praeger Special Studies format will increase its accessibility and that the addition of the 1969 text of the General Agreement will enhance the study of the proposals for trade reform presented in *GATT Plus.*

HENRY H. FOWLER
Chairman
Atlantic Council of the United States

TABLE OF CONTENTS

PART II: TEXT OF THE GENERAL AGREEMENT
ON TARIFFS AND TRADE, 1969

Members of the Special Advisory Panel to
The Trade Committee of the Atlantic Council

Chairman:

Hon. John M. Leddy—Former Assistant Secretary of State and of the Treasury; Former Ambassador to the Organization for Economic Cooperation and Development (OECD); Director, Atlantic Council

Rapporteur:

Mr. Jacques J. Reinstein—Former Government Official; Director, Atlantic Council

Members:

Mr. John W. Evans—Former Government Official and U.S. Representative to the General Agreement on Tariffs and Trade (GATT)

Professor Isaiah Frank—Professor of International Economics, Johns Hopkins University; Former Deputy Assistant Secretary of State and Executive Director, President's Commission on International Trade and Investment Policy

Hon. Theodore R. Gates—Economist; Former Assistant Special Representative for Trade Negotiations

Mr. Mortimer D. Goldstein—Economist; Former Chief of International Finance, Department of State

Hon. Lincoln Gordon—Senior Fellow, Resources for the Future; Former Assistant Secretary of State and President of Johns Hopkins University

Hon. Stanley D. Metzger—Professor of Law, Georgetown University; Former Chairman, U.S. Tariff Commission

Hon. Seymour J. Rubin—Executive Director, American Society of International Law; Former Government Official

Dr. Fred H. Sanderson—Senior Research Fellow, The Brookings Institution

Hon. J. Robert Schaetzel—Former Ambassador to the European Communities; Director, Atlantic Council

Hon. Philip H. Trezise—The Brookings Institution; Former Ambassador to the OECD and Assistant Secretary of State; Director, Atlantic Council

PART
I
REPORT OF
THE SPECIAL
ADVISORY PANEL
TO THE TRADE
COMMITTEE OF THE
ATLANTIC COUNCIL

INTRODUCTION

Classical economic analysis demonstrates persuasively that a well-functioning, competitive international market economy would optimize the use of the world's resources and maximize the total output of goods and services available to meet mankind's needs. We know that this conceptual achievement cannot be fully accomplished even in economic terms. The market works imperfectly and sometimes imposes adjustments upon people or nations which are simply not tolerable without amelioration. In practical political terms, we know that particular nations or groups of nations, and particular industrial or labor groups constantly seek to improve their relative situation or to meet certain social or security objectives by various trade distorting measures. They are not willing to leave their fate solely to market forces.

At least since World War II, the major international trading countries have nevertheless shared a commitment to the principle of a substantially free competitive market as the best means to conduct international trade and serve the best interests of all. Within this context, and primarily through the General Agreement on Tariffs and Trade, these nations have moved toward greater freedom of trade within a set of politically tolerable rules. The trend has been good for the world as a whole. The art has been to meet selectively certain political or humanitarian imperatives even though they derogate from pristine application of classic economic theory and at the same time, to maintain the competitive market as the essence of the international trading system.

The Special Advisory Panel comprised of an exceptionally able and experienced group has developed this report which proposes in thoughtful detail a new initiative for further liberalizing the international trading system. The report is comprehensive and sophisticated. It recognizes and proposes disciplined mechanisms for the realistic compromises that must be entertained in order to give practical life to the basic liberalizing theme. The ideas in the report deserve to be an important part of current international trade negotiations.

LAWRENCE C. McQUADE
Chairman
Trade Committee of the Atlantic
Council of the United States

3

GATT Plus: A Proposal for Trade Reform

The recommendations in this report are directed to the liberalization of world trade and the creation of the new institutional arrangements within GATT needed to give the movement continuing impetus over the years ahead.

The Need and the Way

The Trade Act of 1974 gave the green light to American participation in the Multilateral Trade Negotiations at Geneva, thus opening the way for an important further step in the process of world trade liberalization.

It is the hope that the Geneva negotiations will break new ground in the field of international trade cooperation, including possible supplementary codes for dealing with various nontariff measures. Among the objectives of the negotiations should be the adoption of stronger and better trade rules, better methods of enforcement and improved institutional arrangements. The purpose of this report is to suggest one of the steps that might be taken to contribute to these objectives.

In the Trade Act the Congress directed the President to seek "the revision of decisionmaking procedures in the General Agreement on Tariffs and Trade . . . to more nearly reflect the balance of economic interests."

The thrust of the Congressional policy prescription is right. The decision-making machinery for the international trading system has become inadequate to the trade problems of today and those likely to emerge tomorrow, especially in relations among the advanced industrialized countries which account for the larger share of total world trade. Stronger rules must be established for the conduct and further liberalization of trade among these countries.

GATT is presently the only decision-making body of global scope dealing with international trade problems. Many other world bodies can advise and recommend; but GATT countries, acting as a group, can decide the rights and wrongs of disputes over trade rules, authorize trade retaliation, waive trade obligations, call for consultations, and take many other operative actions. Yet the changes in membership and focus of interest of GATT in recent years have made it increasingly unsuitable as the sole international decision-making institution for the more intensive, yet non-discriminatory, trading relationships which are possible and desirable among the more developed industrialized nations.

Membership in GATT has grown from fewer than 20, mostly industrialized, countries in 1948 to more than 80, mostly developing, countries in 1975. The concern of the developing countries with accelerated industrialization has led to a series of special provisions in GATT rules giving them virtually a free hand to apply trade barriers to protect domestic industries and development programs. The effect of the one-country-one-vote rule has been to give the controlling voice in all GATT decisions, even those affecting trade among the industrialized nations, to countries with a smaller volume of trade and a lesser ability, at their present stage of development, to assume new trade obligations. Under these circumstances the industrialized countries have tended to take their commitments in GATT less and less seriously. An important goal in reform, therefore, should be that decision-making be responsive to the economic weight of the participants.

It is to be emphasized that the essential reforms in the decision-making machinery can be accomplished without depriving the developing countries either of the benefits of the present GATT or of the prospects for improving the condition of their trade. Indeed, the developing countries have a fundamental interest in the expansion of world trade that the further liberalization proposed would make possible.

Modernized trade rules to achieve a substantial further liberalization of trade will require that more decisions be made on an international, rather than on a unilateral or bilateral, basis. And it is the industrialized nations who will have to carry out the reduction of tariffs and nontariff barriers involved.

There is no practical possibility of accomplishing the necessary restructuring through formal amendment of GATT, for example to establish a system of weighted voting for all its members. That would require the consent of two-thirds of GATT's membership and would mean a sharp curtailment in the present voting influence of the developing countries.

The way forward lies in another direction:

- The industrialized nations, acting within the framework of GATT and in furtherance of its objectives, would conclude a supplementary agreement among themselves to liberalize trade in accordance with trade rules tighter than those of GATT and to administer those rules themselves on a weighted-voting basis.

- The trade benefits of the new agreement among industrialized nations would be extended to all GATT countries as required by the most-favored-nation clause.

6

- The agreement would be open to countries which accept common trade rules and would remain open for later accessions. Countries which are developing today could join when they have reached a stage of development where they are no longer in need of special privileges and when they acquire a more direct interest in shaping and contributing to a tighter trading system.

- Relations between the industrialized and developing members of GATT would continue to be handled in accordance with present GATT procedures and voting arrangements and developing countries would retain all their legal trade rights under GATT.

- The new agreement would not impede efforts to resolve differences between industrialized and developing countries on the question of raw materials. It would respect the interests of the developing countries, as recognized by GATT, in cooperative measures to stabilize and improve the conditions of world markets, and in stable, equitable and remunerative export prices for the primary commodities they produce. But arrangements to achieve these objectives should involve participation by both producing and consuming countries on an equitable basis and should not take the form of unilateral restrictive producer agreements.

- The conclusion of this agreement would be sought as one of the results of the Multilateral Trade Negotiations.

New Trade Rules

The agreement among major trading nations would retain the substance of GATT's trade provisions but would alter and supplement particular trade rules to meet current and future problems. The new trade rules would:

- Reduce all import tariffs, across-the-board, by amounts up to 60 percent depending on the height of the duty. Exceptions for specific products by specific countries would be negotiated. The aim of ultimate tariff-free trade should be declared.

- Require that any export restrictions on commodities in short supply, now permitted by GATT, be made subject to prior international consultation. Any such restrictions should treat domestic and foreign consumers on an equitable basis.

- Permit commodity agreements restricting production or trade only if both producing and consuming countries participate equitably in their negotiation and administration.

- Prohibit restrictions or taxes on the export of privately owned

7

technology imposed for the purpose of gaining international commercial advantage.

- Require prior international approval of any plan for the creation of a customs union or free-trade area to assure that it does not provide for preferences in disguise.

- Permit trade preferences by industrialized to developing countries; but prohibit industrialized countries from requiring preferences from developing countries in return ("reverse preferences").

- Permit a new approach to agricultural trade that would bring about gradual changes in domestic farm programs in step with international commitments to reduce the level of protection afforded by these programs. This could be accomplished by a gradual reduction of "margins of support" (*montants de soutien*). Supplemental Agricultural Agreements negotiated for this purpose could also provide for security of access to supplies for importing countries and for internationally coordinated stockpiles to help meet shortages and stabilize prices.

- Prohibit trade measures to cure balance-of-payments problems—whether through import surcharges, import quotas or other devices—unless they have prior international approval, preferably by the International Monetary Fund. But any that do have such approval should be authorized.

- Continue unchanged the "escape clause" of GATT to permit unilateral nondiscriminatory import restraints to prevent "serious injury" to a domestic industry. But "voluntary agreements" to prevent "market disruption" without "serious injury" should be subjected to strict standards of international approval and continuing surveillance.

- Broaden and make more precise existing prohibitions on export subsidies; liberalize "buy-national" government procurement regulations; and establish procedures for future consultation and systematic review of nontariff barriers in general with the aim of preventing new ones as well as curtailing or eliminating old ones.

- Require the explicit listing of any permitted exceptions from basic rules for specific trade practices of specific countries. There should be no "grandfather clause", as in GATT, to conceal such exceptions. Participating countries should be required to certify that they have taken all legal steps necessary to carry out the agreement before signing it.

Organization

The new agreement among major trading nations should be administered within the framework of GATT and financed by special contributions to GATT's budget. Alternatively, it could be brought within the Organization for Economic Cooperation and Development, as was done in 1974 with the International Energy Agency. In either case, provision would be made for the following institutional arrangements:

- A Trade Council (Ministers) and Executive Committee (senior trade officials with policy responsibilities) would be established with votes weighted primarily by importance in world trade. A possible voting pattern for original members would be:

	Trade Votes	Basic Votes	Total Votes	Percentage Distribution of Voting Power
Australia	11.4	4.4	15.8	3.58
Austria	8.9	4.4	13.3	3.01
Canada	39.1	4.4	43.5	9.84
European Community	142.8	4.4	147.2	33.31
Japan	48.5	4.4	52.9	11.97
New Zealand	3.2	4.4	7.6	1.72
Norway	7.4	4.4	11.8	2.67
Sweden	16.1	4.4	20.5	4.64
Switzerland	15.2	4.4	19.6	4.44
United States	105.3	4.4	109.7	24.82
Totals	397.9	44.0	441.9	100.00

- A Director and staff would be provided. The Director would chair the Executive Committee and have the right to initiate proposals for action.
- The Director-General of GATT would be invited to participate in meetings of the Trade Council and Executive Committee.
- Periodic reports would be made to the whole GATT membership. Also, the Executive Committee would create a Consultative Group to receive views from GATT countries, particularly developing countries, not participating in the agreement.
- The Trade Council would establish procedures for receiving views from private business, labor, agricultural, consumer and other groups and individuals on trade barrier problems.

- The Trade Council would have all necessary powers to interpret the trade rules, adopt new rules of a supplementary kind to meet changing conditions, conduct consultations and suspend trade obligations temporarily when justified.

- A participating country complaining of damage to its trade because of the violation of the trade rules by another would be able to require a prompt decision by the Executive Committee on the rights and wrongs of the matter. If no decision were forthcoming within a prescribed time limit, the complaining country would be free to suspend equivalent trade obligations, on a discriminatory basis, against the trade of the offender. The use of panels of independent persons in helping to settle disputes would be encouraged. These procedures would correct serious inequities and deficiencies in the present GATT enforcement system.

A Code of Trade Liberalization

The trade rules and institutional arrangements sketched above would be incorporated in a comprehensive Code of Trade Liberalization. An illustrative text with a commentary follows.

PROPOSED CODE OF TRADE LIBERALIZATION
Commentary and Text

General Concept of Code

The proposed Code of Trade Liberalization would constitute a new trade agreement among major trading nations designed to: (1) liberalize trade through the substantial further reduction of tariffs and other trade barriers, (2) tighten and improve existing GATT trade rules along more equitable lines, and (3) provide a more effective international enforcement mechanism for trade commitments than is now available under GATT. The trade benefits of the Code would be extended to all GATT countries by virtue of GATT's most-favored-nation (MFN) clause. The Code would not require discrimination against any country.

Thus, the Code would supplement GATT and reinforce GATT's trade objectives. GATT would remain the major world forum for trade relations between those GATT nations which accept the Code and those which do not. Because the developing countries are today unable to accept even the existing obligations of GATT in full, but must have recourse to the broad exceptions granted them by Article XVIII and Part IV of GATT, it is not expected that they would be able to accept the more extensive obligations of the Code. But if a developing country should achieve in the future a stage of development enabling it to accept the Code in full, it should be encouraged to do so.

Code obligations would be enforced exclusively by those nations which adhere to it, in accordance with the principle of equity that only those countries which accept common obligations should be entitled to interpret and assure their effective application. Trade relations between Code members and other contracting parties of GATT would continue to be enforced through GATT.

The various provisions of the Code are inter-related. In particular, the trade rules of the Code should be read in the light of the enforcement provisions of Section XII and the institutional provisions of Section XV which differ sharply from the comparable provisions of GATT.

The annotated outline of the proposed Code which follows provides an illustrative text for each section of the Code preceded by a background commentary.

11

ESTABLISHMENT PROVISION
Establishment of Code in Furtherance of GATT Objectives

Commentary

The illustrative text of the "Establishment Provision" shown below is self-explanatory except possibly for two points. First, it is intended to be on the same legal footing as the rest of the Code and is not preambular or hortatory in nature. Second, the undertaking in paragraph 3 by each member to "collaborate with the organs of the Code" is designed to be a source of legal authority for the institutions of the Code.

Illustrative Text

The Governments and the Council of the European Community, on whose behalf this Code is signed, agree as follows:

1. A Code of Trade Liberalization (hereinafter called the "Code") is hereby established in furtherance of the objectives of the General Agreement on Tariffs and Trade (hereinafter called "GATT") and shall be carried out in accordance with the following provisions.

2. The term "members" means those on whose behalf this Code is signed and which are represented in the Trade Council and the Executive Committee under the provisions of Section XV of the Code.

3. Each member undertakes to collaborate with the organs of the Code to further the liberalization of international trade and to eliminate unfair international trade practices.

SECTION I
Application of GATT Trade Rules

Commentary

The Code would accept the existing trade rules of GATT as the basic commercial policy framework to be strengthened and improved by the Code. These trade rules are set forth in Articles I through XVII and XIX through XXIV of GATT and related notes and supplementary provisions and include, for example, the most-favored-nation clause and permissible departures from it such as customs unions and free-trade areas, tariff commitments, the application of internal taxes and regulations, the use of import and export quotas, safeguard provisions (the "escape clause"), and many others relating to various nontariff trade barriers. The Code would not, however, permit the use of the broad exceptions granted by GATT to developing countries (Article XVIII and Part IV of GATT) nor would it incorporate various organizational and similar non-trade provisions in GATT. The Code would provide its own arrangements regarding organization, interpretation and enforcement, withdrawal, etc.

The purpose of the illustrative text shown for Section I is to establish that basic GATT trade rules would henceforth be applied by Code members in the improved form called for by other sections of the Code, and would be enforced exclusively by Code members in their trade relations with each other. Any "waivers" of trade rules carried over from GATT to the Code would have to be specifically listed in the Waivers Annex to the Code. No attempt has been made to suggest a text for the Waivers Annex.

Trade relations between Code members and other GATT countries not members of the Code would continue, as before, to be governed by GATT.

Illustrative Text

1. Members of the Code undertake to apply in commercial relations among themselves Articles I through XVII and XIX through XXIV to GATT (together with Annex I and such other Annexes to GATT as are relevant for members and are still in force) in accordance with, and subject to, the other provisions of this Code. Wherever the term "contracting party" is used in GATT, it shall be understood for the purposes of the Code to mean a "member" of the Code; and wherever the term "CONTRACTING PARTIES" is used in GATT, it shall be understood to mean for the purposes of the Code the members of the Code acting through the Trade Council and Executive Committee as provided for in Section XV of the Code.

2. Articles XVIII, XXV through XXXV and Part IV of GATT shall not be construed to modify the rights and obligations of members established by the Code.

3. Waivers granted by the CONTRACTING PARTIES pursuant to Article XXV of GATT prior to the effective date of this Code shall not apply to the obligations described in paragraph 1, above, unless they are specifically listed in the Waivers Annex to this Code, which is made an integral part thereof.

SECTION II
Reduction of Tariffs

Commentary

Two distinct techniques for the reduction of tariffs by international agreement have emerged in the postwar period.

The first, or "selective" method, involves the negotiation of each tariff item separately, product-by-product, with the extent of the tariff reduction granted varying from tariff item to tariff item. This is the method that has been normally used in GATT negotiations. The end result is reflected in Article II of GATT and the tariff schedules annexed to the Agreement. Article II of GATT provides that products specifically listed in a country's schedule "shall be exempt from ordinary customs duties in excess of" those stated in the schedule and from "all other duties or charges" in excess of those in effect at the time.

The second method of tariff negotiation requires the reduction of duties across-the-board by a stated percentage or percentages, with any exceptions to the rule specifically stated and agreed upon. The across-the-board method is the one which has been used by Western European countries in eliminating tariffs within the European Community, among the members of the European Free Trade Association, and between the EC and individual members of EFTA. For example, the agreement between Switzerland and the EC (1972) contains in Article 3 of that agreement the simply stated proposition that all industrial products, with the exception of certain products listed and described in the agreement, shall be eliminated in five yearly installments of 20 percent each. The Swiss-EC agreement covers some 90 percent of all trade between them.

European countries have often advocated the across-the-board method of tariff reduction in GATT negotiations. But it was not until the Kennedy Round (1963-67), the latest of the six rounds of GATT tariff negotiations, that an important step was taken in this direction. The negotiators accepted the objective of a flat 50 percent reduction of the then-existing tariffs on products of which other participating countries were principal suppliers as a "working hypothesis" of the negotiations. This, of course, left wide latitude for negotiating different reductions for many products. It is estimated that the Kennedy Round resulted in an average reduction of about 35 percent.

The illustrative text suggested below for inclusion in the proposed Code of Trade Liberalization would establish the application of across-the-board tariff reduction as an international legal requirement, and not merely as a "working hypothesis". Room would be left for the inevitably necessary exceptions, which would have to be specifically agreed upon and listed in annexes. The pattern proposed for achieving an across-the-board reduction is within the authority granted the President by the Congress of the United States in the Trade Act of 1974. This pattern, applied across-the-board, would have several advantages. It would reduce higher tariffs more than lower tariffs, thus creating greater equity both among national tariff systems and, within any given national system, among different products. It would make visible and understandable to citizen and lawmaker alike the extent to which reciprocity had been achieved.

It should be emphasized that the pattern of across-the-board tariff reductions suggested in the text below is only one of several possibilities; a variety of other useful approaches to tariff reduction could be formulated.

The tariff reductions resulting from the Code would be extended to all GATT countries by virtue of GATT's most-favored-nation clause (GATT's Article I). In other words, *so long as the Code tariff reductions were in effect*, GATT countries not members of the Code would be entitled to them. However, such countries could not prevent Code members from altering the Code tariff rates proposed below so long as the principle of nondiscrimination is observed. Members of the Code would, for example, reserve to themselves the right to refuse to apply the tariff reductions in Section II of the Code on products principally supplied by developed countries which, although fully able to do so, refuse to accept the obligations of the Code. This would be essential to assure reciprocity.

Since the point is often misunderstood, it should be emphasized that the withholding of a tariff reduction in respect of a *product principally supplied by* a non-joiner does not entail discrimination against the non-joiner; the tariff reduction simply would not be made to any supplier of the product so long as the major beneficiary of the tariff reduction, the "principal supplier", refuses to join.

All GATT countries, including members of the Code, would however, retain all their legal rights to the tariff treatment provided for in GATT itself as a result of earlier tariff negotiations, and these earlier GATT legal rights would be incorporated in the Code by virtue of Section I of the Code described elsewhere.

Neither the illustrative text shown below nor other provisions suggested for the Code would permit easy or periodic increases in tariff rates as now provided for by GATT's Article XXVIII. Article XXVIII is not one of the GATT Articles proposed for inclusion in the Code. Individual tariffs could, however, be increased above the ceilings specified by the Code if (1) the Trade Council approves by a majority of the votes cast, and (2) that majority includes all members of the Code having a substantial interest as suppliers of the product concerned.

"Tariff Annex 1" referred to in paragraph 3 of the text below is intended to permit a more precise translation of the maximum duties and timetables into the customs language of the members than is possible in the general provisions of the Code. The reference to "Tariff Annexes Nos. 2 through _____," in paragraph 4 of the text relates to the exceptions for particular products of particular countries. No attempt has been made to suggest a text for the Tariff Annexes.

Illustrative Text

1. An objective of the Code shall be to achieve, in time, the elimination of the customs tariffs of the members. As a first step toward the achievement of this objective, members shall apply the following provisions of this Section.

2. Except as provided in paragraph 3 of this Section, products imported into the territory of any member which are the products of any other member shall, upon their importation, be exempt from most-favored-nation ordinary customs duties in excess of the duties described below, and shall be exempt from all other duties and charges of any kind imposed on or in connection with importation in excess of those imposed on January 1, 1975, or those directly and mandatorily required to be imposed thereafter by legislation in force in the importing territory on that date:

   (a) No rate of duty existing on January 1, 1975, including zero rates of duty, shall be increased.

   (b) If the rate of duty existing on January 1, 1975, is not more than 5 percent *ad valorem*, it shall be eliminated over a period of not more than two years.

   (c) If the rate of duty existing on January 1, 1975, is more than 5 percent *ad valorem* but not more than 10 percent *ad valorem*, it shall be reduced to 5 percent *ad valorem* over a period of not more than two years.

   (d) If the rate of duty existing on January 1, 1975, is more than 10 percent *ad valorem* but not more than 20 percent *ad valorem*, it shall be reduced to 8 percent *ad valorem* over a period of not more than 4 years.

   (e) If the rate of duty existing on January 1, 1975, is more than 20 percent *ad valorem*, it shall be reduced to not more than 40 percent of the rate existing on January 1, 1975, over a period of not more than 10 years.

   (f) No member shall be required by the provisions of subparagraphs (c) or (d) of this paragraph to reduce the rate of duty on any product to a rate below 40 percent of the rate existing on January 1, 1975.

3. The maximum rates of duty provided for in paragraph 2, above, shall be applied in accordance with the detailed rules and timetable described in Tariff Annex No. 1 to this Code, which is made an integral part thereof.

4. The exceptions to paragraph 2, above, shall be those specified in Tariff Annexes Nos. 2 through _____, which shall also state the maximum tariff rates applicable to the named products in the territories of the members concerned. These Annexes are made an integral part of this Code.

5. The principles of paragraphs 2, 3, 4 and 5 of Article II of GATT shall also apply to the import tariff obligations of members under this Code.

6. The Trade Council may, by a majority of the votes cast, authorize a member to increase the rate of duty on any product above the maximum rate provided for by paragraph 2 of this Section, above, if the majority of votes

cast includes the affirmative votes of all members having a substantial interest as suppliers of the product concerned.

7. If a developed contracting party to GATT fails to adhere to the Code within a reasonable period after its entry into force, or if a member of the Code ceases to be a member, the Trade Council may authorize any member to suspend the application of the provisions of this Section to products principally supplied by that contracting party or former member. The Trade Council may make regulations for carrying out the provisions of this paragraph.

SECTION III
Access to Supplies and Technology

Commentary

GATT's provisions indicate little concern over the problem of access to supplies and none at all over access to technology. Only recently has public attention turned to product shortages and some of their longer-term implications. The notion of imposing governmental restrictions on the international transfer of private technology is also a recent one, advanced mainly in the hope of restraining international competition and without much consideration for the broader consequences of such action in encouraging the wasteful use of economic resources.

What GATT says about product shortages is briefly this:

— Any country confronted with a critical shortage of foodstuffs or other essential products may restrict, or even prohibit, exports of the product without international consultation or concern for the needs of other countries (Article XI, paragraph 2(a)).

— Any country may adopt any trade measure to conserve an "exhaustible" natural resource if there are restrictions on domestic production or consumption. International consultation is not required (Article XX, paragraph (g)).

— Any country may limit exports of materials in order to assure essential quantities to a domestic processing industry if the domestic price is held below the world price by a stabilization plan. Consultation is not required, and the only limits are that the restrictions may not discriminate among countries and may not operate to increase the protection or exports of the domestic processing industry (Article XX, paragraph (i)).

— Any country may take any measure "essential to the acquisition or distribution of products in general or local short supply", but in this case the principle of equitable sharing must be observed although no international consultation is required. A provision of this

17

general kind was included in the original GATT but was supposed to terminate after the immediate post-war period. For obscure reasons it was continued in the revised form quoted above in subsequent GATT amendments as paragraph (j) of Article XX.

— Any country may impose export taxes or charges without consultation or limit because GATT says nothing to prevent it.

In addition, GATT's Article XX, paragraph (h) would permit intergovernmental commodity agreements restricting production and exports. As has been shown most dramatically in the case of oil, such agreements negotiated by producers can be used to create world shortages of the most serious kind and not merely to relieve the distress caused by heavy surpluses and extremely low prices. By means of an interpretative note to this GATT provision referring back to an old U.N. ECOSOC (Economic and Social Council) Resolution of 1947, which endorsed various criteria then being discussed in the context of the International Trade Organization (ITO) Charter, the GATT provision can be construed to require equitable representation in such agreements by consuming as well as producing countries. On the other hand, the language of the GATT provision would permit any commodity agreement, or criteria for commodity agreements, submitted to GATT and "not disapproved" by it. Thus, a majority of the GATT countries, most of which today are developing countries whose leaders favor commodity agreements to support the prices of their raw materials and tropical foodstuffs, could easily decide "not to disapprove" a particular producer agreement or even producers' agreements in general so long as they benefit developing countries and regardless of their effects on others. While the Code cannot in the short run alter the views of the developing countries on this issue, it is important that the major trading countries make clear in the Code their own view that commodity agreements are not acceptable trade devices unless both producers and consumers are adequately represented in their negotiation and administration.

The central purposes of that part of the illustrative text shown below which relate to shortages are three: (1) to assure advance international consultation or agreement before trade measures are used to meet shortage situations; (2) to assert the principle of equitable international sharing in such cases; and (3) to encourage the development of positive and constructive programs, rather than restrictive trade measures, to cope with shortage problems over the longer term, especially in the field of non-renewable resources. In addition, the illustrative text would require, insofar as participation by Code members is concerned, that commodity agreements reflect both consumer and producer interests. With respect to prior consultation with the Trade Council on trade measures to meet shortages, the Trade Council, under Section XV of the Code, would be authorized to establish procedures assuring the confidentiality and rapid conclusion of such consultations.

The question of agriculture and shortages, including the use of stockpiles, is treated later on at length in Section VI of the Code.

The illustrative provision included in the text below on the subject of access to technology is intended to stop, before they start, incipient national movements to keep technology at home, either for protectionist reasons or to gain preferential commercial advantage within the international trading system. At the moment few if any countries restrain the international transfer of technology for other than security reasons, a situation which is worth preserving.

Illustrative Text

1. No prohibition or restriction on the export or sale for export of any product applied by any member pursuant to paragraph 2(a) of Article XI or to paragraphs (g) or (i) of Article XX of GATT shall be applied to the export or sale for export of any product destined for the territory of any other member, nor shall any tax, duty or other charge be newly imposed or, if now imposed, increased by any member on the export or sale for export of any product destined for the territory of any other member, except after consultation through the Trade Council. Any such prohibition, restriction, tax, duty or charge shall be administered consistently with the objective of assuring the equitable sharing of scarce supplies between essential domestic and foreign requirements, taking into account the shares prevailing in a prior representative period and any special factors affecting the trade in the product concerned. Any member applying a trade measure pursuant to this paragraph shall remove it as soon as the circumstances giving rise to its application shall have ceased to exist.

2. Each member affirms that any measure it may adopt pursuant to paragraph (j) of Article XX of GATT as being essential to the acquisition or distribution of a product in general or in local short supply shall be consistent with the principle of the equitable international sharing of the supply of that product. If any member proposes to adopt any measure, or proposes to enter into an international agreement, to assure to itself access to a product in short supply, it shall first consult through the Trade Council with respect to the consistency of the proposed measure or agreement with the above principle.

3. The members affirm that concerted intergovernmental measures to restrict production or trade in any product for the purpose of limiting its international supply or maintaining or increasing its international price must take the form of an intergovernmental commodity agreement providing for equitable representation by consuming and producing countries alike in the negotiation and administration of the agreement. Accordingly, members agree

that in their commercial relations with each other they will apply the following provision in lieu of paragraph (h) of Article XX of GATT:

"(h) undertaken in pursuance of obligations under any intergovernmental commodity agreement which provides for equitable participation by both consuming and producing countries;"

4. In the event of a continuing shortage, however caused, of the international supply of a non-renewable resource, the members shall, upon the request of any of them, consult through the Trade Council, GATT, the Organization for Economic Cooperation and Development, or any other appropriate international institution, regarding the best means of increasing the supply or reducing the demand of the non-renewable resource, including measures designed to increase or share the existing supply, develop alternative or substitute sources of supply, alter patterns of consumption or improve technology. Any measures adopted pursuant to this paragraph and having the approval of the Trade Council may be applied by any member notwithstanding other provisions of this Code.

5. No member shall prevent, limit or tax the export on a commercial basis of privately-owned technology to the territory of another member. This paragraph shall not prevent any member from imposing a charge on the export of such technology in order to recover the costs of governmental research and development if the charge is no higher than that made for the same technology when sold domestically on a commercial basis. This paragraph shall not prevent measures applied in respect of technology for the moral, health or enforcement purposes described in paragraphs (a), (b) and (d) of Article XX of GATT or those taken for the essential security interests described in Article XXI of GATT.

SECTION IV
The Use of Quantitative Restrictions

Commentary

Quantitative restrictions are defined in GATT as prohibitions or restrictions on trade "other than duties, taxes or other charges" and are understood to mean absolute limits on the quantity or value of a product permitted to be imported or exported. Prohibitions are flat embargoes. Restrictions are implemented either by published quotas setting the maximum physical limit of a product, whether measured by volume or value, which may be imported or exported during a given period, or by import or export licensing to accomplish the same purpose, or both. It is safe to assume that if a government requires a permit or license *as a condition of importation or exportation* it is applying a quantitative restriction whether or not the government claims to be granting licenses "freely."

GATT's Article XI contains a general prohibition on the use of quantitative restrictions (paragraph 1) but lists several exceptions. The first of these, relating to export restrictions to relieve critical shortages of foodstuffs (paragraph 2(a)) was discussed in Section III, "Access to Supplies and Technology."

The second exception in Article XI, paragraph 2(b), permits restrictions to enforce standards or regulations for the classification, grading or marketing of commodities in international trade. This exception, although reasonable in intent, is liable to abuse through the use of definitions for the purpose of restricting trade rather than to assure proper descriptions or classifications in setting standards. But nontariff barriers of this kind can best be winkled out through complaint procedures or highly specific international agreements supplemental to GATT or to the Code. Section X of the proposed Code outlines a mechanism for encouraging supplemental agreements on nontariff barriers.

Paragraph 2(c) used to be GATT's most important exception, so far as developed countries are concerned, to the rules against quantitative restrictions, apart possibly from the latitude given for their use for balance-of-payments purposes. It permits import restrictions on any agricultural or fisheries product if domestic production or marketing is controlled, or to get rid of a temporary surplus in cases where partial cut-rate sales are made of the domestic product, and in certain highly specialized situations involving domestic restrictions on animal products. For the reasons stated in Section VI of the proposed Code relating to agriculture, these elaborate provisions have become obsolete, and a fresh approach to the problem of agricultural trade is required.

The illustrative text below would accomplish two things: (1) It would eliminate licensing systems other than those required to enforce quantitative restrictions permitted by the Code. (2) It would eliminate the exception for agricultural products, leaving this question to be dealt with in Section VI of the Code. The basic rule of GATT's Article XI, paragraph 1, prohibiting quantitative restrictions in general would remain, together with the minor exception for standards under paragraph 2(b) plus the exception for shortages in paragraph 2(a) as revised by Section III relating to access to markets and technology.

Illustrative Text

1. No member shall require licenses or permits as a condition for the importation of any product of the territory of any other member or for the exportation of any product destined for the territory of any other member except for

the purpose of enforcing prohibitions or restrictions authorized under the provisions of this Code.

2. Members shall, in their commercial relations with each other, adhere to the provisions of Section VI of the Code in lieu of the provisions of paragraph 2(c) of Article XI of GATT insofar as that paragraph relates to agricultural products.

SECTION V
Equality of Trade Treatment

Commentary

The basic principle of equality of trade treatment is set forth in paragraph 1 of Article I (the unconditional most-favored-nation clause) of GATT. The same principle is adapted to various kinds of nontariff barriers elsewhere in GATT, notably in the provisions dealing with import and export quotas and internal taxes and regulations affecting trade. The unconditional most-favored-nation principle has a long history, has been amply tested by experience and, when fully applied, gives effective legal and practical expression to equality of trade treatment.

GATT recognizes several exceptions to the requirement of equality of trade treatment, some hoary with age, some new.

First, there are the preferential residues of the break-up of the old imperial and colonial systems and other historical associations. These may be retained under GATT but cannot be increased and must be reduced as most-favored-nation tariffs are reduced (GATT's Article I, paragraphs 2 and 4). After six rounds of tariff negotiations these preferences can be said to be of minimal importance except for a few commodities.

Second, there are customs unions and free-trade areas (GATT's Article XXIV, paragraphs 5 through 10). Customs unions have been a standard exception from the most-favored-nation clause almost since its birth. Free-trade areas are relatively new, having been first introduced during GATT negotiations in the early postwar period. The essential difference between the two is that in a customs union the external tariffs (and other external trade regulations) of the parties to the union must be identical or nearly so whereas in a free-trade area each partner may keep its own external tariff and trade regulations. In both cases there is supposed to be complete (or nearly complete) free trade among the partners. The economic rationale for both is similar: that free internal trade among the partners will have sufficient expansionary effects on trade with the outside world to more than offset the depressing trade effects of the differential trade treatment accorded outsiders. In short, the trade-creating effects overall are believed to more than offset the trade-diverting effects. But there is also a political rationale for customs unions which does not hold for free-trade areas. This is that the customs union is essential to full economic integration, which in turn is essential to the political union of previously sovereign states. The classic case is the 19th century German *Zollverein,* which preceded the creation of the German nation.

GATT also provides for "interim agreements" leading to the formation of a customs union or free-trade area "within a reasonable length of time." Both the definition of the degree of internal free trade required in customs unions and free-trade areas and the likelihood of the ultimate fruition of an interim agreement, especially the latter, leave considerable latitude for international argument. GATT provides that all of these arrangements be subject to scrutiny by GATT but requires that the CONTRACTING PARTIES positively disapprove an interim arrangement already agreed upon before it must be changed to meet GATT's criteria and requirements. In other words, failure of GATT to act against a *fait accompli* is, in effect, GATT consent. In this way several purely preferential arrangements dressed up in the language of interim agreements for customs unions or free-trade areas or "association" agreements—notably between the European Community and developing countries in Europe, Africa and the Middle East—have slid through without a GATT finding one way or the other. The economic and political objections to these lie not so much in the preferences accorded to the developing partners (which ought, nevertheless, to be accorded also to other developing countries) but in the "reverse preferences" which the developing partner is required to give the developed partner in return. The European Community has recognized this problem and in the trade and aid agreement signed at Lomé, Togo, in February 1975 agreed with 46 developing countries in Africa, the Caribbean and the Pacific not to require reverse preferences favoring the Community's exports as a condition of the preferences and aid to be accorded these countries by the Community.

The third class of exceptions to the most-favored-nation clause consists of those permitted to facilitate frontier traffic between adjacent countries and those accorded by contiguous countries to the Free Territory of Trieste (GATT's Article XXIV, paragraphs 3(a) and 3(b)). Both of these are beneficial and noncontroversial.

Finally, there are the waivers for specific preferential arrangements that have been granted by a two-thirds vote of the GATT CONTRACTING PARTIES under Article XXV, paragraph 5. No attempt is made here to review these waivers but it may be noted for American and Canadian readers that the U.S.-Canadian Automotive Agreement is the subject of one of them.

The illustrative text shown below would not attempt to sweep away all old preferences or change the basic concepts of the customs union or free-trade area. Three alterations in GATT provisions are proposed:

1. Future interim agreements for customs unions or free-trade areas would be made subject to the prior approval of the Trade Council, which would have to give it, however, if the criteria for these arrangements were truly met. In other words, an international body would have to give positive approval to make the arrangements legal; whereas in GATT the arrangement stands unless GATT acts negatively.

2. Existing or future two-way preferential arrangements between developed and developing countries (whether or not in the guise of customs unions or free-trade areas or something else) would have to be converted into one-way arrangements by enabling developing countries to eliminate the "reverse preferences" they have been required to give developed countries. Nevertheless, certain existing doubtful cases may have to be accommodated for overriding political considerations if for no other. Accordingly, an exception to the general rule would be permitted if specifically exempted and recorded in the Code at the time of signature.

3. The text would not prevent trade preferences by members to developing countries and to their dependent territories. However, it would not relieve members of their GATT obligations regarding preferences to developing countries not members of the Code (see commentary and text of Section XI).

In addition, it is proposed that GATT waivers from the principle of equality of trade which have been granted to signatories be reviewed in the course of negotiating the Code and that those which it is agreed to continue would be specifically listed in the Waivers Annex (see Section I).

Illustrative Text

1. No member shall maintain or enter into an interim agreement leading to a customs union or free-trade area without the prior approval of the Trade Council. The Trade Council shall grant such approval if it finds that the

proposed interim agreement meets the conditions and requirements set forth in paragraphs 5(a), 5(b), and 5(c) of Article XXIV of GATT. (Note: any exception for a specific existing arrangement from the requirements of this paragraph would have to be agreed upon before signature of the Code and recorded in an Annex to it.)

2. The Trade Council may adopt regulations for the observance and administration of the provisions of paragraph 1, above, which paragraph, together with any regulations adopted by the Trade Council, shall supersede the provisions of paragraph 7 of Article XXIV of GATT in commercial relations among members.

3. No member which is party to an interim agreement for a customs union or free-trade or other preferential or discriminatory arrangement with a country which claims in respect of that member privileges comparable to those accorded to developing countries under Article XVIII or Part IV of GATT shall invoke its legal claims under such interim agreement or other preferential or discriminatory arrangement, nor shall it apply or threaten measures of trade retaliation or other economic sanction, to prevent the developing country from according full equality of trade treatment, as defined in Article I, and in other provisions of GATT, to the trade of any other member.

4. This Section shall not prevent any member from extending, without reciprocity, preferences to the trade of any developing country or to that of any territory, not a part of its customs territory, for which it has responsibility.

SECTION VI
Agriculture

Commentary

For many basic agricultural products GATT's techniques for liberalizing trade have been inadequate almost since the beginning. The special rule in GATT permitting import quotas on agricultural products only when the domestic product is also subject to an equivalent form of control or intervention (Article XI, paragraph 2(c)) broke down almost immediately after GATT's signature. In the early 1950s the United States Congress legislated import quotas on dairy products even though no limits were placed on the domestic dairy industry as required by GATT. It then directed that GATT not be allowed to stand in the way of any import restrictions necessary to prevent interference with a domestic farm program of any kind. This is believed to be the only instance on record where the Congress has specifically ordered the President to violate trade-agreement commitments. The United States accordingly sought a waiver from GATT, which was reluctantly granted. The waiver remains in force today. Later, when the European Community was formed, the same problem arose in Europe. The Common Agricultural Policy (CAP), which was and is an essential part of the Community, took the form of extensive governmental intervention in the setting of farm prices, accompanied by variable levies on imports of competing products, and, in some cases, export subsidies. Thus for several basic farm products Community agriculture has been effectively isolated from the world market. The Community has avoided conflict with Article XI of GATT limiting the use of import quotas on agricultural products by adopting a system of variable import levies which are permitted under Article II of GATT for products on which no tariff concessions are granted. In the Kennedy Round the Community negotiated successfully for the withdrawal of previous tariff bindings by member states on products for which variable levies were planned.

It seems clear from this history, as well as from similar situations in other developed countries, that the methods for expanding trade by conventional techniques which are limited to trade-barrier commitments will not work for a number of basic agricultural products. Almost all developed countries have a long history of political and social concern for the place of the farmer in their industrialized societies. This concern has been expressed through domestic programs designed to bolster farm incomes in relation to other incomes and to protect home farmers against the risks of extreme fluctuations in price and production. Domestic programs for these purposes usually involve government intervention in the market which may take the form of: (1) market price supports implemented by government purchases or guarantees usually requiring corresponding import restrictions or fees and often export subsidies; (2) price deficiency or supplement payments; (3) surplus disposal programs; and, in some cases, (4) acreage or production restraints. But, whatever the form, the usual experience has been that once a domestic program has been established and embarked upon, international trade commitments that would permit foreign trade to interfere with the domestic program have been brushed aside, or, as noted in the case of the European Community, avoided.

Further efforts to negotiate trade-barrier commitments for major agricultural products *without clear understandings concerning consequential changes in the domestic programs likely to affect those products* would prove as futile in the future as they have in the past. A fresh approach is therefore needed.

Because of persisting difficulties in reconciling domestic agricultural programs with international trade policies writers sometimes treat the subject as though all of "agriculture" had been written out of GATT. This would not be accurate. A large number of agricultural products move in international trade on the same GATT terms as nonagricultural products. Although many of these agricultural products are not of great individual importance, together they comprise a substantial volume of international trade. For the most part these products do not pose special problems and the conventional type of trade commitment can be applied to them in the future as in the past.

The problem in devising a new approach to agricultural trade is how to bring about gradual changes in domestic farm programs in step with international commitments to reduce the level of protection which such programs afford against international competition. The problem may not be insoluble but is surely difficult. Farm policies are set by the play of domestic political forces, often expressed through legislative acts; trade agreements are negotiated by other officials in a different context.

In negotiating changes in domestic agricultural programs, an effort should be made to reconcile the basic objectives of these programs—improved incomes, particularly of low-income farmers, security of supplies and price stability—with the objective of increased economic efficiency through expanded trade. Furthermore, countries should not be required to dismantle existing techniques of support or protection provided their overall protective effect is gradually reduced.

In view of different conditions in the various agricultural commodity markets, it will be necessary to deal separately with some of the major commodities or groups of commodities of prime importance in international trade such as wheat, feed grains, meat, dairy products, sugar, and possibly oilseeds, cotton and tobacco.

The illustrative text below provides a framework that would accommodate a differentiated approach for these sectors which would link international trade negotiations with consequential changes in related domestic farm programs in a gradual, evolutionary process. Specifically named agricultural products to which domestic programs apply would be exempt from the general trade rules regarding tariffs, and quotas (but would not be exempt from the rules regarding nondiscrimination or access to supplies except for commodity agreements pursuant to Article XX paragraph (h) of GATT). These products would be specifically listed in an Agricultural Annex to the Code agreed upon at the time of its signature but could be added to later by action of the Code's Trade Council (see Section XV on institutions of the Code).

It is assumed that the Agricultural Annex to the Code would

specify, among other products: wheat, feed grains, meat, dairy products, sugar, and possibly oilseeds, cotton and tobacco. These commodities would appear to meet the criteria of agricultural products for which conventional trade-barrier commitments alone would be inadequate. For products listed in the Agricultural Annex to the Code, members would agree to negotiate "Supplemental Agricultural Agreements," each Agreement setting forth specific assurances regarding the product concerned. For a minimum number of these products—for example, wheat, feed grains, dairy products and meat—Supplemental Agricultural Agreements should be concluded simultaneously with conclusion of the Code of Trade Liberalization itself. International assurances regarding such an important segment of world trade would seem essential to any true reform of the international trading system. Internationally coordinated stockpiles of these products could make an important contribution to stabilizing supplies and prices.

For farm products which are not materially affected by domestic programs and not specifically singled out for special exemption in the Agricultural Annex, the ordinary rules of GATT, as changed by the Code, would apply.

The Supplemental Agricultural Agreements could provide for one or more of several kinds of international understandings:

(1) Commitments to carry out a phased reduction of margins of support (*montants de soutien*), defined as the difference between the price received by the domestic producer and an "international reference price." The international reference price would not be an actual market price but a "best estimate" of the long-term equilibrium price in the world market. The difference between the domestic producer price and the international reference price would reflect the effects of tariffs, variable levies, import quotas and export subsidies in raising domestic prices. Domestic producer prices would include not only the price received by producers on the domestic market but any product-specific subsidies such as price support (deficiency) payments (but not general subsidies such as research and extension services, input subsidies, social welfare-type payments, adjustment assistance). Domestic producer prices and international reference prices would be adjusted for transportation costs to major ports of export, for exporting countries, and major ports of entry, for importing countries. International reference prices would be reviewed from time to time, for example every two years, in the light of market developments but would remain fixed in the intervals, except for possible automatic adjustments to allow for world-wide inflation of

28

production costs. In effect, the scheme would leave governments free to provide price guarantees for one or more production cycles—subject, however, to a long-term schedule of step-by-step reductions of the margins of support. So long as these margins were observed, the form of implementing the permissible level of protection or support, whether through price intervention, tariffs, levies or fees, import quotas or export subsidies, price deficiency payments, production, acreage or marketing restrictions, or any combination of these, would not be in question. *

(2) Agreement to encourage programs to deal with the problems of low-income farmers by (a) income supplement grants and (b) adjustment assistance to enable marginal farmers to earn additional income from non-farm sources or to give up farming altogether.

(3) Provision for coordinated stockpiles subject to international guidelines and consultations and financed through national or international funding, to help in avoiding shortages and ensuring greater stability of international prices.

(4) In order to better assure security of access to supplies for importing countries and security of access to markets for exporting countries, the establishment of rules stricter than the general rules of the Code concerning the imposition, administration and phasing out of any temporary export or import restrictions; and possibly minimum import and export commitments within an agreed price range.

(5) Commitments for international food aid and understandings concerning the terms and conditions of such aid, including provisions to safeguard normal commercial trade.

(6) Commitments on maximum self-sufficiency ratios.

(7) Commitments with respect to conventional trade barriers, i.e., setting the level of permissible tariffs or levies, use of quantitative restrictions, export subsidies and the like.

Provision could be made, either in the Agricultural Annex, or in a Supplemental Agricultural Agreement, specifying in detail the trade treatment to be provided for an agricultural product in the event a Supplemental Agricultural Agreement is not concluded simultaneously with the entry into force of the Code, or is not renewed, or is terminated. Such trade treatment could include the re-establishment of previously existing rights and obligations regarding the product concerned.

An illustration of how the margin of support proposal might work in specific cases is given in Appendix B of this report.

To summarize: the illustrative text below reflects the need for explicit international recognition of the distinctive problems of farm communities and would establish a formal basis for their serious international discussion. It would stress the importance of gradual structural farm adjustment, for helping to improve farm incomes and for widening access to both international markets and supplies. It would call for immediate concrete agreements for certain agricultural products of prime importance in international trade to be concluded for relatively short initial periods with continuing adjustments and renewals in the light of changing conditions. Finally, since some international agreements for some agricultural products would require for their effectiveness the participation of producing or consuming countries which might not be in a position to accept the entire Code, it would envisage the participation of those countries in specific agricultural agreements.

Illustrative Text

Part A
Applicability of Code Trade Provisions
to Certain Agricultural Products

1. Agricultural products shall be exempt from the provisions of Section II of the Code and of Article II of GATT, as incorporated in the Code, insofar as these provisions limit charges on imports other than ordinary customs duties, and Article XI of GATT as incorporated in the Code, but shall be subject to the provisions of Section VI of the Code, if:

  (a) Such agricultural products are or become subject to internal governmental measures or programs that operate to support domestic agricultural prices or incomes, to control domestic production, acreage or marketing, or to manage domestic surpluses or supplies, which internal governmental measures or programs would be seriously endangered by the failure to apply trade measures inconsistent with the provisions of the Code and GATT referred to in paragraph 1 above; and

  (b) Such agricultural products are specified in the Agricultural Annex to the Code, either on the effective date of the Code or by later approval of the Trade Council; and subject to such conditions as may be stated in the Annex.

2. Agricultural products of the members which are not subject to Section VI of the Code shall be subject to all of the other provisions of the Code.

3. Notwithstanding the provisions of paragraph 1, above, if a prohibition, restriction, tax, duty or other charge is applied by any member on the export or sale for export of any agricultural product (whether or not subject to the provisions of Section VI of the Code) destined for the territory of any other member, the principles of paragraph 1 of Section III of the Code shall apply.

Part B
Supplemental Agricultural Agreements

1. Adequate intergovernmental assurances to further the stability and growth of international trade in the agricultural products specified in the Agricultural Annex are an essential part of the understandings among members embodied in the Code. Accordingly, members undertake to provide such assurances through the conclusion and periodic renewal of Supplemental Agricultural Agreements for products specified in the Agricultural Annex. The objectives of such agreements shall include the achievement of mutually advantageous understandings regarding:

(a) the adjustment of the internal measures or programs referred to in paragraph 1(a) of Part A of this Section (or alternatively commitments with respect to conventional barriers to international trade in the products subject to such measures or programs) in such a way as to enable the gradual widening of opportunities for international trade in the agricultural products concerned;

(b) measures to assure security of access to supplies for importing countries and security of access to markets for exporting countries, including the establishment, where appropriate, of internationally coordinated stockpiles to help in meeting shortages and stabilizing international prices; and

(c) the encouragement of structural adjustments in agriculture to improve and stabilize the income of farmers while enabling production and sales to meet the requirements of expanding consumption at reasonable prices.

2. Supplemental Agricultural Agreements may include participation by governments not members of the Code and may provide for the administration and operation of such agreements separately from the institutions of the Code in accordance with procedural and voting arrangements agreed upon by the participants in such agreements.

3. Members of the Code participating in a Supplemental Agricultural Agreement or engaged in negotiations for the conclusion of such an agreement shall, upon the request of any member of the Code, or upon the request of the Trade Council, consult with the Trade Council regarding the effect of the agreement or proposed agreement on the trade of members in the light of the objectives required of such agreements by the provisions of paragraph 1, above, of Part B of this Section.

SECTION VII
Trade Measures Relating to the International Monetary System

Commentary

The right of a country to impose restrictions on its merchandise trade in order to protect its balance of payments is currently limited by two substantially different sets of rules: one, in the Articles of Agreement of the International Monetary Fund, applies to exchange restrictions on payments for imports; and the other in GATT applies to quantitative restrictions (QRs) on imports. Which one applies to a given situation may depend on the form of the restriction rather than its substance or its consequences for other countries. Thus, a restriction that is administered by the banking or foreign exchange system is ordinarily considered by the Fund to be within its approval jurisdiction; a similar restriction administered by customs officials is ordinarily deemed subject to GATT's jurisdiction.

The Fund Agreement (Article VIII) prohibits, without *prior* Fund approval, the imposition of restrictions on current payments and transfers, including payments for imports. The exchange restrictions covered by this prohibition include exchange quotas, exchange licensing requirements, multiple currency practices, and exchange taxes. The Fund considers each case on its merits.

The "transitional period" provisions (Article XIV:3) of the Fund Agreement provide for an exception to the rule of Article VIII for a country unable to accept its full obligations under the Agreement. That exception, which is not applicable to a country that has established a convertible currency (i.e., generally, the industrialized countries) allows for the maintenance, but not the initiation, of exchange restrictions on current payments without Fund approval.

Members maintaining exchange restrictions consult annually with the Fund. A member that maintains restrictions that are inconsistent with the Fund's purposes may lose access to the Fund's resources and ultimately be expelled.

GATT, on the other hand, allows a country to introduce or intensify quantitative import restrictions (QRs) to safeguard its external financial position and balance of payments without prior approval or prior consultation (Article XII:1 and, for developing countries, Article XVIII:9). Consultation with GATT is required as soon as possible after QRs are imposed; the Fund participates in the consultation and provides a determination on the financial position of the restricting country (Article XV:2). Consultations are also required annually with an industrialized country, and biennially with a developing country, maintaining QRs.

GATT requires that QRs be non-discriminatory with respect to exporting countries (Article XIII), except in certain specified circumstances (Article XIV), and meet specified commercial policy standards (Article XII:3 (c)).

If the CONTRACTING PARTIES to GATT find that a country

is maintaining QRs inconsistently with GATT, they may, after going through specified procedural steps, release an injured country from particular GATT obligations.

GATT makes no provision for imposing import surcharges (the trade analogue of exchange taxes on imports) for balance-of-payments purposes. Such measures may be imposed without violating GATT's tariff commitments only if GATT grants a waiver. A number of countries—both industrialized countries and less developed countries—have nevertheless chosen to use import surcharges, rather than exchange restrictions or QRs, to protect their external financial positions. GATT, similarly, makes no provision for the use of export subsidies for balance-of-payments purposes although the Fund may approve a multiple currency practice for that reason.

The existing Fund/GATT system in this area has operated in an arbitrary manner and has produced results that are not desirable. A country that wants to exercise direct control over imports, and finds it administratively and politically feasible to operate quantitative import restrictions, can introduce them without prior approval of the Fund or consultation with anyone; or if it decides to violate its tariff commitments under GATT, it can impose import surcharges. Sometime later it must face a Fund finding in GATT, but in circumstances where the Fund's concern is less than direct and immediate, its inclination to do battle is ordinarily restrained, and its power virtually impossible to utilize. On the other hand, a country that cannot use a trade control mechanism but must operate through the exchange system is subjected, properly, to prior examination.

The illustrative text that follows is designed to remedy these defects. It would establish a single rule—prior approval—for the imposition of any form of direct governmental measures designed to safeguard a member's balance of payments, thus extending to trade measures the prior approval principle now applicable to exchange measures. "Trade measures" embrace quantitative import restrictions, which are now permitted by GATT for balance-of-payments purposes, and import surcharges and export subsidies, whose use for such purposes is not currently permitted by GATT.

Prior approval could be given by the International Monetary Fund, if the present jurisdiction of the Fund is broadened to cover trade measures to safeguard the balance of payments. If the jurisdiction of the Fund is not so broadened, then the approval could be given by the Trade Council, after consultation with the Fund. Similarly, the application of trade measures could be authorized under the Fund Agreement for the purpose of limiting transactions with a country whose currency is deemed "scarce" in accordance with Article VII of that agreement. To avoid speculation in the private market, the Trade Council, under Section XV of the proposed Code, would have authority to establish regulations assuring the confidentiality and rapid conclusion of discussions between a member and the Council.

The changes proposed here would not relieve a member of the Code of its obligation to adhere to the principles of commercial policy specified in Article XII:3(c) of GATT in the administration of quantitative import restrictions.

A special word needs to be said about the application of import surcharges (and export subsidies) for balance-of-payments reasons. The proposed Code would permit these measures (for example, instead of QR's) but they could well conflict with a Code member's GATT obligations to a non-member. For this reason, the illustrative text below provides that Code members should take the legal steps open to them to modify these obligations (e.g., through tariff renegotiation, a GATT waiver, etc.).

Illustrative Text

In their commercial relations with each other, members shall apply the following provisions in lieu of Articles XII, XIV, and XV of GATT:

1. Nothing in this Code shall prevent any member from applying import restrictions or other trade measures for the purpose of safeguarding its balance of payments and reserve position if such action:

(a) has been approved by the International Monetary Fund pursuant to the Articles of Agreement of the Fund or pursuant to an arrangement between the Fund and the members of the Code, or is otherwise authorized by the Articles of the Agreement of the Fund; or

(b) has been approved by the Trade Council.

2. The Trade Council shall be empowered to make decisions in accordance with clause (b) of paragraph 1 of this Section only if it finds that clause (a) is of no effect because the International Monetary Fund is not empowered to approve the application of trade measures and the Articles of Agreement of the Fund do not otherwise authorize the application of trade measures. If the Trade Council so finds, it shall seek an agreement with the Fund respecting participation by the Fund whenever the Trade Council is considering the approval of trade measures pursuant to clause (b).

3. With respect to trade measures applied by a member pursuant to clause (b) of paragraph 1 of this Section, the Trade Council may specify a schedule of consultations between the Trade Council and the member, requirements for the progressive relaxation of such measures, a date for the expiration of its approval, and any other conditions it considers to be appropriate. With respect to trade measures applied pursuant to clause (a), the Trade Council may require consultations between the Trade Council and the member concerning

the administration of such measures, and, pursuant to arrangements with the International Monetary Fund, may participate in consultations between the Fund and the member.

4. Within 30 days after the Trade Council convenes, each member shall notify the Trade Council of the trade measures it is applying for the purpose of safeguarding its balance of payments and reserve position. As soon as possible, the Trade Council shall make a determination pursuant to paragraph 2 of this Section whether it may proceed in accordance with clause (b) of paragraph 1 of this Section and, if so, shall decide whether the trade measures so notified shall be approved. Pending a decision pursuant to paragraph 1, trade measures so notified shall not be deemed inconsistent with the provisions of the Code.

5. A member applying import restrictions under paragraph 1 of this Section shall administer them in accordance with the principles of paragraph 3(c) of Article XII of GATT.

6. No member shall invoke the provisions of Article II or Article XVI of GATT to prevent the application by another member of import surcharges or export subsidies applied pursuant to paragraph 1 of this Section, and each member shall take such legal steps as may be open to it to modify any of its international obligations to non-members which might prevent such application.

7. The Trade Council shall seek cooperation with the International Monetary Fund to the end that the Trade Council and the Fund may pursue coordinated policies, within their respective jurisdictions, in furtherance of their common objectives.

SECTION VIII
Subsidies, Countervailing Duties, Dumping and Antidumping Practices

Commentary

Subsidies, countervailing duties and antidumping practices are among the nontariff barriers to international trade often cited in current studies as being in need of greater international restraint. They are also among the nontariff trade barriers which have received the most discussion internationally and are the subject of some of the more complex and elaborate provisions of GATT.

Subsidies

All "subsidies" given by a GATT member, "including any form of income or price support," which operate to increase exports or reduce imports must be reported to GATT and, if the subsidy "prejudices" the interests of another member, the member granting the subsidy must, if asked, discuss "the possibility of limiting" it with the other affected member or with GATT. (Paragraph 1, Section A, of GATT's Article XVI). Since governments are reluctant to volunteer that they may be granting a subsidy—especially one that may hurt another country—the GATT Secretariat has developed the habit of sending around a general questionnaire to the GATT countries every two or three years. Most of GATT's industrialized members, but few of its developing members, respond to this questionnaire in some fashion.

Export subsidies are carved out of the area of subsidies in general and subjected to additional and more stringent rules. If the subsidized product is a "primary product," that is an agricultural, fishery or mineral product, export subsidies are discouraged (paragraphs 2 and 3, Section B, Article XVI) but are permitted so long as they do not result in the subsidizer getting "more than an equitable share of world export trade" in that product (paragraph 3, Section B, Article XVI). Most controversies in GATT concerning these subsidies have related to agricultural primary products. As noted later on, there is also a question of definition here in the case of semi-processed primary products. For the reasons given in the commentary for Section VI of the Code dealing with agriculture, it is believed that more effective rules governing the use of both general and export subsidies in the case of agricultural products of major importance in world trade and clearly falling within the category of "primary products" can best be accomplished through "Supplemental Agricultural Agreements" for each of the products concerned.

If the product is *not* a primary product, and the export subsidy "results in the sale of such product for export at a price lower than the comparable price charged for the like product to buyers in the domestic market," it is prohibited (paragraph 4, Section B, Article XVI). This prohibition was added to GATT, after a long and tortuous process, by a supplemental instrument (a "Declaration") to which almost all of the industrialized market-economy countries but very few developing countries now adhere.

All of the countries, except Australia, which are tentatively listed in Section XV of the proposed Code as being probable initial members of the Code have accepted the Declaration prohibiting export subsidies on non-primary products. It is understood that Australia has felt that so long as the rules against export subsidies on primary products were so lax it would have to remain free to subsidize exports of non-primary products.

The existing provisions of GATT dealing with subsidies are unsatisfactory; there are serious loopholes as well as ambiguities and inconsistencies. At no point does GATT define the word "subsidy." As a result of case law, there is general agreement on one element that must be present for a practice to constitute a subsidy: it must involve a cost to the government. At the same time there is no subsidy if the exported product is exempt from taxes borne by the like product when destined for domestic consumption (Interpretative Note to Article XVI, Annex I). A number of questions are left open. When is relief from a direct (income) tax or the deferral of such a tax to be considered a subsidy? Is any expenditure by Federal or local authorities that lowers the cost or increases the profitability of producing goods to be considered a subsidy (for example, the donation by government of the results of research and development expenditures without cost to the producer)? Are governmental practices subsidies when they have the same effect as subsidies, but do not result in a direct or indirect payment to the producer or exporter (for example, the practice of providing loans for the development of foreign markets that are excused if the venture fails)?

The definition of an export subsidy is also deficient. The provision dealing with export subsidies on primary products appears to apply to any subsidy "which operates to increase the export of [a product] from its territory. . ." This phrase would cover a wide range of subsidies usually considered to be domestic.

GATT has made several attempts to define the export subsidies on non-primary products prohibited by paragraph 4 of Article XVI. A 1960 GATT Working Party Report contained a partial list of kinds of measures believed to fall under the prohibition, including the payment of direct subsidies to exporters, the exemption from or refund of direct (income) taxes or social welfare charges conditioned on exportation, and various kinds of government financial assistance to exportation such as credit guarantees at below-market interest rates. The Working Party did not specify whether the examples on its list were subject to the further qualification that the existence of dual-pricing must be shown before they are prohibited. The Working Party reported that the countries applying the export subsidy prohibition were "generally agreed" on this partial list, but it would be hard to say what the international legal status of the Working Party's examples is or how they actually affect the specific actions or practices of the governments which have agreed to the prohibition.

Finally, in view of the difference in GATT provisions related to subsidies on primary and non-primary products, the dividing line between the two is important. The text of GATT (one of the Interpretative notes in Annex I) states that a primary product must be "in its natural form or [have] undergone such processing as is customarily required to prepare it for marketing in substantial volume in international trade." There is considerable room for difference of opinion as to what degree of processing is required before the product ceases to be a primary product and therefore falls under the prohibition of export subsidies on non-primary products of Article XVI, paragraph 4.

Most of these problems have been subject to lengthy discussion in a series of working groups in GATT preparatory to the Multilateral Trade Negotiations (MTN), and, since early 1975, have been the subject of actual negotiation. Many proposals are being considered in these negotiations, mostly in the direction of tightening the commitments against trade-distorting export incentives. It is suggested that any improvements in the definitions of subsidies, primary products and export subsidies which can be agreed upon in the Multilateral Trade negotiations, at least so far as developed countries are concerned, should be incorporated in the proposed Code of Trade Liberalization, together with certain procedural improvements described at the close of this commentary.

Countervailing Duties

There is little symmetry between GATT provisions governing the use of subsidies and those that govern the use of countervailing duties by an importing country. A countervailing duty may be imposed against imports of any product that has benefited from any kind of subsidy, even if it is not an export subsidy that is prohibited or limited by GATT. On the other hand, the importing country, before imposing a countervailing duty, must satisfy itself that the subsidy is causing or threatening material injury to a domestic industry or materially retarding its establishment (paragraph 6(a) of Article VI).

There is solid reason for requiring that an "injury" test be used before applying countervailing duties: the uncertainty surrounding the question whether a governmental practice does in fact constitute a "subsidy" with an attendant distortion of international trade such that a countervailing duty is justified to remove the distortion. There is the danger of overcountervailing, of creating a greater distortion of trade than the alleged cause.

There is less of a case for requiring an injury test before countervailing export subsidies prohibited by international agreement (paragraph 4 of Article XVI) simply because automatic countervailing in such cases, without the need to demonstrate injury, could help to ensure observance of the prohibition. But here again, the problem of

38

definition, while less slippery, is by no means automatic or certain. It is suggested in the proposed Code that the injury test could be dispensed with as a condition for applying countervailing duties in cases in which the Trade Council has determined that the subsidy is in fact an export subsidy prohibited by the Code. For this purpose, and also to lessen some of the international controversy that has attended the use of countervailing duties as well as subsidies, it is proposed that the Code also require a member to consult with the Trade Council before imposing countervailing duties.

It should be noted that until the enactment of the Trade Act of 1974, United States' countervailing-duty law did not provide for an injury test. The conflict with GATT's Article VI was saved by the "grandfather clause" of GATT described in the commentary on Section XIII of the Code. In the Trade Act of 1974 an injury test was prescribed, but only for countervailing duties against imports of duty-free products, all of which have hitherto been exempt from countervailing duties under U.S. law. The Congressional reasons for this curiously differential treatment appear to have been three: (1) Congress wished to extend the countervailing-duty law to products newly placed on the free list, especially as a result of the generalized system of tariff preferences to developing countries also authorized by the Trade Act of 1974; (2) it wished to avoid deliberate violation of a GATT rule from which the United States was not saved by the "grandfather clause"; and (3) it hoped that other countries could somehow be brought to pay, in reciprocal concessions, for any action by Congress in the future to enable the United States to abandon the protection of the "grandfather clause" by extending the injury test to all products.

Under the original GATT the countervailing (or antidumping) duty could be levied only by the country importing the product. A country whose exports faced the competition of subsidized or dumped products in third markets had no redress except the possibility of a successful complaint in the case of a subsidy which violated Article XVI. Later on an attempt was made to ameliorate the problem; GATT may now authorize—but not require—the third country receiving the dumped or subsidized products to impose the duty to prevent injury to the exports of another party.

This change in GATT rules has not solved the problem. Such action by GATT has never been requested, and the issue of injury to exports to third markets from export subsidies continues to be a source of contention. It is believed that this situation would be improved under the proposed Code because of the new procedures suggested for enforcement of the Code which would, so far as members are concerned, replace the old "nullification or impairment" procedures of GATT's Article XXIII. Under the proposed new enforcement system it would be possible for an exporting member, A, damaged by a prohibited export subsidy granted by another member, B, on exports to some third country, C, to take direct action against the trade of B through a speeded-up and definitive procedure. Reliance on action by C, which experience has shown to be virtually hopeless, could be dispensed with. For a description of these procedures, see Section XII of the Code.

Dumping and Antidumping Practices

The subject of dumping is more simply dealt with. The GATT definition of dumping (paragraph 1 of GATT's Article VI) is clear cut and is generally accepted, as is the right of an importing country to levy antidumping duties.

The principal difficulties which have arisen in this area relate to the manner in which governments administer their antidumping laws: the extent to which interested parties are permitted to testify before the administrative authorities, the issuance of adequate information, the restriction of imports (or suspension of appraisement) pending sometimes onerously protracted delays in reaching a decision, and the extent to which there is strict observance of the requirement that dumped imports cause material injury to a domestic industry.

During the Kennedy Round an Antidumping Code was negotiated and accepted by all major industrialized countries. The Code gives greater precision to the provisions of Article VI and commits participants to fuller disclosure, opportunity for interested parties to express their views, and generally accelerated and streamlined procedures. The proposed Code of Trade Liberalization would incorporate the substantive articles of the Antidumping Code of GATT without disturbing certain of its organizational provisions which involve participation by several countries—e.g. Finland, Greece and Yugoslavia—that could not be expected to accept the obligations of the Code of Trade Liberalization, at least for a considerable period of time.

It will be recalled that all of GATT's provisions on subsidies, countervailing duties and antidumping duties would be incorporated in the proposed Code by virtue of Section I of the Code. The illustrative text for Section VIII shown below would, in summary, supplement or alter these provisions in the following ways:

—The prohibition against subsidies on exports of non-primary products of GATT's Article XVI, paragraph 4, would be replaced by the clearer and more detailed definition of prohibited export subsidies which it is hoped will emerge from the Multilateral Trade Negotiations at Geneva. In the event that the Geneva negotiations should result in an entire new code on subsidies, or on subsidies and countervailing duties, the substance of that code could, of course, be included in the proposed Code of Trade Liberalization; although it is believed that the procedural improvements suggested below should be retained in any event.

—The Trade Council would be authorized to ask for, and get, full information from members on their specific actions or practices which the Council believes may be subsidies and to define particular actions or practices, or kinds of actions or practices, as either general subsidies or export subsidies.

—Members would be required to consult the Trade Council well in advance of imposing a countervailing duty. If the Council found that a particular subsidy was a prohibited export subsidy, the member countervailing it would not have to meet the injury test.

—The Code would incorporate the substance of the Antidumping Code along with the basic antidumping provisions of GATT.

Illustrative Text

1. Members shall apply the following provisions in lieu of paragraph 4 of Article XVI of GATT:

(Note: This would list the new, detailed definitions of prohibited export subsidies which it is hoped will emerge from the Geneva Multilateral Trade Negotiations, at least insofar as developed countries are concerned.)

2. Members shall, upon the request of the Trade Council, provide it with all information available to them regarding specific governmental actions or practices of a member which the Council believes may constitute a subsidy in terms of any provision of Article XVI of GATT as incorporated in the Code. The Council may, for the purposes of the Code, define specific actions or practices of a member, or kinds or classes of actions or practices of members generally, as constituting such subsidies.

3. Any member considering the imposition of a countervailing duty on the importation of a product of another member shall, not less than 120 days prior to the imposition of such duty, notify the Trade Council and shall promptly consult with such other member and, upon request of the Trade Council, with the Council. In any case in which the Trade Council determines that the product is being exported with benefit of an export subsidy prohibited by the terms of paragraph 1 of this Section, the member considering the imposition of a countervailing duty on such product shall not be required to make the determination regarding material injury to domestic industry referred to in paragraph 6(a) of Article VI of GATT.

4. In their commercial relations with each other, members shall apply the antidumping provisions of GATT as interpreted and elaborated by Articles 1 through 12 of the Agreement on Implementation of Article VI of the General Agreement on Tariffs and Trade of June 30, 1967.

SECTION IX
Safeguard Provisions

Commentary

Article XIX of GATT, the "escape clause" provision, allows a GATT country, notwithstanding other commitments of GATT, to impose restrictions, increase tariffs or apply other trade measures to limit imports which cause or threaten serious injury to domestic producers of the like or directly competitive product. A country resorting to the escape clause must notify and consult with other affected countries. Also, it must in all cases adhere to the rule of nondiscrimination in applying any trade measure to imports. In practice, the notification requirement has been met by notifying the GATT Director-General of the proposed action; and the consultation requirement by a procedure resulting in either compensatory trade concessions by the import-restricting country or withdrawal by the adversely affected exporting country of substantially equivalent trade concessions, thus balancing the accounts.

Article XIX has been invoked relatively infrequently, partly no doubt because "no significant industries have anywhere been overwhelmed by import competition".* Also, the necessity for raising duties or imposing import quotas on a nondiscriminatory (most-favored-nation) basis as a remedy, with compensation to all other GATT countries adversely affected, may have been a deterrent.

The various limitations on the use of the escape clause, however, have played a significant role in the proliferation in recent years of "voluntary arrangements" to curtail imports, bypassing the standards set by Article XIX. In the cases of large industries such as textiles and steel, as well as some smaller ones, there have been rapid percentage increases in imports from a particular country or a group of countries within a relatively short period of time, sometimes called "market disruption," which motivated the negotiation of trade restraints not subjected to domestic and international escape clause procedures.

While voluntary arrangements have been brought under GATT's aegis in one case (textile products) and made subject to certain multilateral rules and surveillance, others have not. No agreed principles exist concerning the circumstances under which such arrangements should be permitted; the forum in which they should be scrutinized

---

*Trilateral Commission, Directions for World Trade in the Nineteen Seventies (1974), p. 24.

before and after they are negotiated; whether and in what form compensation should be accorded to countries adversely affected; their duration; whether and in what degree upward adjustments of permitted export levels should be provided for during the period when the arrangement is in effect; whether a country which induces such export restraints must undertake domestic measures, either general or specific, which would help its affected industry to adjust; or whether such voluntary arrangements may be administered on a discriminatory basis, i.e., exclusively against imports of "low-wage" developing countries, or those of particular developed countries which have increased exports quickly and in large quantities.

The illustrative text shown below would leave Article XIX undisturbed but would establish principles and procedures relating to voluntary arrangements of a restrictive nature which would govern such arrangements as among two or more Code members. Unlike Article XIX, such arrangements would not have to meet a "serious injury" test. Since most voluntary agreements are implemented by foreign exporters, strict technical observance of the most-favored-nation rule would not be required. However, the arrangement would have to apply to all major suppliers of the product concerned unless the Trade Council, by a qualified majority, decided otherwise.

Among other things, the illustrative text shown below is designed to prevent unilateral action by a major trading country to pressure individual suppliers, including weaker nations, into unwarranted restrictive actions.

It should be noted that the phrase "appropriate domestic adjustment measures" in paragraph 3 (c) is intended to include broad measures with general effects on the domestic economy and not to be limited to "adjustment assistance".

Illustrative Text

Members shall observe the following provisions supplementary to those of Article XIX of GATT incorporated in the Code pursuant to paragraph 1 of Section 1 of the Code:

1. No member shall enter into or facilitate an intergovernmental or other international voluntary or other arrangement for the application of trade measures which limits import competition, whether by export restraints or otherwise, with its domestic producers unless such arrangement shall have been approved by the Trade Council in accordance with the provisions of paragraphs 3 and 4 below.

2. The Trade Council shall, not later than two years after the entry into force of the Code, review, in the light of the requirements for arrangements

43

set forth in paragraphs 3 and 4 below, arrangements existing on the date of the entry into force of the Code. If the Council disapproves such an existing arrangement, the arrangement shall be terminated forthwith.

3. The Trade Council shall not approve an arrangement proposed to be concluded after the entry into force of the Code, unless it is convinced that the arrangement is warranted by unusual circumstances affecting the trade of the importing member, including:

(a) a large increase in imports has occurred over a short period of time affecting adversely an industry which is of substantial importance to the economy of the country desiring to restrict imports; and

(b) such industry has not been capable of adjusting to such import competition during that period of time; and

(c) the member desiring to restrict imports has initiated a process of adopting appropriate domestic adjustment measures.

4. Such an arrangement proposed to be concluded after the entry into force of the Code shall not be approved by the Trade Council unless it is satisfied that:

(a) the initial levels of permitted imports are not less than those which occurred during a recent representative period, and upward adjustments in the levels of permitted imports are provided for periodically during the time the arrangements are in force, in appropriate proportion to anticipated or actual increases in domestic consumption; and

(b) appropriate compensation or withdrawal of concessions, as the case may be, is afforded or made available to members adversely affected thereby, unless in special circumstances the Trade Council, by a two-thirds majority of the votes cast, finds that such compensation or withdrawal is not appropriate;

(c) import-limiting measures are applied in respect to all members which are substantial suppliers of the product concerned on a most-favored-nation basis, unless in special circumstances the Trade Council finds, by a two-thirds majority of the votes cast, that the general application of such measures is not appropriate;

(d) the duration of any arrangement is limited to three years, with any renewal subject to approval by the Trade Council as if it were an original arrangement.

5. During the existence of any arrangement approved by the Trade Council, under paragraphs 1 or 2, above, the Trade Council shall hold annual consultations for the purpose of determining the extent to which the arrangement meets the conditions set forth in paragraphs 3 and 4, above.

6. Any Code member may at any time request the Trade Council to hold consultations concerning the application of an arrangement which the Trade Council has approved, in which event the Council shall convene a consultation within thirty days of the request. The Council may withdraw its approval of the arrangement following any consultation pursuant to this paragraph if it finds that the conditions of paragraphs 3 and 4 are not being met, in which event the arrangement shall no longer be of any force and effect.

SECTION X

Nontariff Barriers: Procedures for the Future

Commentary

The term "nontariff barriers" appears in the title of this Section, and elsewhere in the commentary, out of deference to the wide practice in current writing of using it in the condemnatory sense of all forms of governmental intervention, other than the ordinary tariff, designed to tip the scales of international competition in favor of domestic producers or consumers to the disadvantage of those abroad. In fact there are many "nontariff barriers" to trade which do not have this purpose or effect and which are entirely justifiable. Prohibitions on trade in articles made from endangered species, for example, are surely not objectionable. Many others of longer standing could be cited which are warranted on grounds of public policy despite their interference with trade. Also, the term "nontariff barriers" as commonly used includes direct subsidies to domestic industries as well as various cost measures against imports such as import surcharges, fees and levies and discriminatory internal taxes which in fact are tariff or tariff-like in that they are money payments exacted exclusively in relation to the imported product. Because of its imprecision the term "nontariff barriers" is not used in the illustrative text shown below. Instead, paragraph 1 of the illustrative text defines what is objectionable, and deserving of curtailment, elimination or prevention, as "policies and practices, other than ordinary customs duties, which introduce inequities or distortions into the international trading system to the benefit of domestic producers or consumers and to the disadvantage of foreign producers or consumers."

As explained elsewhere, all of GATT's many rules governing nontariff barriers would be incorporated in the Code, some of them in improved and strengthened form; new rules would be added; and all trade rules would, under the Code, be subject to more effective enforcement procedures than is, or can be made, available in GATT. Moreover, under the Code all exceptions to the rules would have to be out in the open and could no longer be hidden by GATT's "grandfather clause" (see commentary on Section XIII of the Code).

International negotiations have been actively pursued in recent years on two important types of nontariff barriers in respect of which no attempt has been made to suggest rules for the proposed Code: product standards and government procurement.

The making and enforcement of product standards can create significant obstacles to international trade. GATT establishes the principle that "all laws, regulations and requirements affecting . . . internal sale, offering for sale, purchase, transportation, distribution or use" shall apply to imported and domestic products on the same basis, i.e. without discrimination (GATT's Article III, paragraph 4). But this principle of national treatment is not stated precisely enough to reach into and control the numerous and highly complex systems—mandatory and voluntary, public and private—for establishing product specifications and assuring that particular products meet those specifications. A GATT Working Party has prepared a draft of a special code designed to accomplish this control on an international basis, and it is hoped that reasonably prompt agreement can be reached on an acceptable draft during the current Multilateral Trade Negotiations in Geneva. The standards code would be a comprehensive one—the draft comprises some thirty closely printed pages covering all significant aspects of the problem. No judgment can be expressed here on the technical adequacy of the text under negotiation. A standards code should attract membership at the outset from many developing countries which would stand to gain as they produce more industrial goods. It is not recommended that the proposed standards code should become a part of the Code of Trade Liberalization, or even that it should be fully integrated into GATT. Rather it should be an autonomous instrument within the framework of GATT administered by those governments that participate in it. Once basic policies have been established, the rules regarding product standards should be administered by those with specialized technical knowledge in industrial processes not usually possessed by the commercial policy officials who attend GATT meetings or who might be expected to administer the proposed Code of Trade Liberalization.

The administration of government purchases to favor domestic producers is no doubt one of the oldest forms of governmental assistance to national economic, especially industrial, development. What is surprising is that this costly practice has persisted, despite periodic international efforts to suppress it, in countries which have long since become fully industrialized. An early postwar attempt to rule out "buy-national" practices was a total failure because of the opposition of almost all major trading nations. As a result, government procurement of products "purchased for governmental purposes and not with a view to resale or with a view to use in the production of goods for commercial sale" is completely exempt from the rules requiring that internal measures treat foreign and domestic products alike (GATT's

Article III, paragraph 8 (a)). Also, by cross-reference, such government procurement is exempt from GATT's unconditional most-favored-nation clause (GATT's Article I, paragraph 1). Thus members of GATT may, in government procurement matters, freely discriminate both against foreign products in general and against particular foreign suppliers.

Work has been underway for some time in the OECD on a "Draft Instrument" to eliminate buy-national practices. Like the product standards code in GATT, the draft instrument is intended to be comprehensive, setting forth detailed rules regarding government purchasing policies, procedures and practices which would assure, to the maximum extent practicable, application of the principle of nondiscrimination against the products or nationals of countries participating in the instrument. OECD's technical work on a government procurement code is of high quality and well in hand. The central question is whether the major trading nations of the OECD will agree to it. It is recommended that in order to reach agreement, the instrument should be linked to progress in the Multilateral Trade Negotiations at Geneva. It is also recommended that, if agreement can be reached, the basic rules regarding procurement be incorporated in the proposed Code of Trade Liberalization. It should be noted that since government purchasing is exempt from the most-favored-nation clause, the benefits from any new rules establishing national treatment could be limited to the countries which were prepared to apply the new rules, i.e. the "conditional" form of the most-favored-nation clause.

Even assuming complete success in current international trade negotiations, including adoption of a standards code, a code on government procurement, and the proposed Code of Trade Liberalization, there would still remain many nontariff barriers (of the objectionable kind) that may be expected to yield only to patient international discussion and negotiation over many years. Of equal, if not greater, importance is the prospect that new kinds of barriers will be considered by governments in the future. New policies will be required to meet changing economic conditions. A new emphasis is already being placed on the quality of life, including improvement of the environment, with attendant economic costs and trade effects. And there may emerge, at least in some countries, what certain European officials and writers call "industrial policies", i.e. national policies involving governmental intervention on a more extensive basis than is found in today's industrial market economies.

The illustrative text below is directed to these two problems: (1)

assuring a continuing effort by major trading nations to eliminate or reduce remaining nontariff barriers and (2) establishing an international surveillance and consultation procedure to prevent the emergence of new barriers which might otherwise be unilaterally created in the future.

Paragraph 1 of the illustrative text is intended as a declaration of common interest in mitigating or doing away with a defined class of existing trade policies and practices and preventing new ones. The definition is that given at the beginning of this commentary.

The second paragraph of the illustrative text calls for prior international notification and consultation regarding possible new barriers, and it should be noted that here the definition is substantially narrower than that in paragraph 1 since it would be limited to measures by a member "which would apply to the product of another member . . . or to the export of a domestic product." In other words, the requirement of prior notification and consultation would not extend, for example, to the many forms of subsidy or assistance given to domestic producers (although notification and consultation *post* would continue to be required in the case of domestic subsidies as explained in the commentary on Section VIII of the Code). Even so, paragraph 2 is a broad one; and for this reason provision is made in paragraph 3 for the Trade Council, by majority vote, to establish regulations for its application, including rules for waiving prior notification and consultation in emergencies. (A more highly qualified vote would otherwise be required for a waiver under Section XV of the Code). Paragraph 2 would not come into force until a year after the Code came into force, thus giving the Trade Council time to work out its regulations.

The fourth and last paragraph of the illustrative text of this Section adapts to the trade field a procedure which has worked reasonably well in the OECD for macro-economic policies and in the IMF (and GATT) for balance-of-payments policies: that of systematic and periodic national reviews. Here the definition of what is to be reviewed is broader than those of either paragraphs 1 or 2, and would embrace "policies and practices which affect the conditions of international competition." This breadth of definition is necessary if the reviews are to cope with new or future trade problems of the kind described earlier. At the same time, there is no intention that these national reviews should duplicate what is now being done by the OECD for national economic policies or the IMF for monetary policy.

Illustrative Text

1. The members affirm their common interest in achieving the curtailment or elimination of existing policies and practices, other than ordinary customs duties, which introduce inequities and distortions into the international trading system to the benefit of domestic producers or consumers and to the disadvantage of foreign producers or consumers, and in preventing the adoption of new policies and practices of this kind in the future. They undertake to collaborate with the organs of the Code in furtherance of these objectives.

2. Subject to the provisions of paragraph 3 of this Section, any member considering the adoption of a measure which would apply to a product of another member, whether or not it would also apply to the like domestic product, or which would apply to the export of a domestic product, shall notify the Trade Council prior to making such measure effective and shall, if requested by another member, or by the Trade Council, consult with the other member or the Council, as the case may be, regarding (a) the consistency of the proposed measure with the obligations under the Code of the member considering the adoption of the measure and (b) whether or not the measure is consistent with such obligations, any adverse effect it may have on the trade of the other member. This paragraph shall enter into force upon the expiration of one year after the entry into force of the Code.

3. The Trade Council may, by regulation approved by a majority of the votes cast, establish rules for the application of paragraph 2 of this Section, including rules for waiving the requirement for prior notification and consultation in emergency circumstances.

4. The Trade Council shall, within two years after the entry into force of the Code, establish a system for the periodic, intensive review of the policies and practices of each member, whether or not such policies or practices are consistent with the member's obligations under the Code, which affect the conditions of international competition. Members shall provide the Trade Council with all information necessary for the effective conduct of such reviews. In the light of such reviews the Trade Council may, in accordance with the provisions of Section XV of the Code, make recommendations to members, adopt supplemental codes or take other appropriate action in furtherance of the objectives stated in paragraph 1 of this Section.

SECTION XI
Relationship of Code to Certain Other Multilateral Trade Arrangements

Commentary

Since the Code is designed to achieve a greater degree of trade liberalization than GATT rules, and also to extend the liberalized treatment to all GATT countries without discrimination, the possibility that a member of the Code might be required by it to take trade action contravening the member's trade obligations to non-member GATT countries is unlikely. Nevertheless, to allay any suspicions on this score, it is as well to make explicit the fact that members of the Code would not be required to violate their GATT trade commitments to other countries in order to carry out the Code.

Also, it is desirable to provide for periodic reporting to GATT on the operation of the Code and a consultative mechanism to assure that trade problems, especially of developing countries, raised by GATT countries not members of the Code, would be taken into account by the institutions of the Code.

A second set of problems, of a different order, arises from the recent birth of two new multilateral arrangements affecting trade: the Geneva textile arrangement concluded under GATT in 1973 and the International Energy Program and Agency concluded under the OECD in 1974. Both of these involve restrictive trade measures which could raise questions concerning their consistency with the Code's trade rules. The textile arrangement is clearly a protective device designed to accomplish a purpose similar to that of the "escape clause" or "gentlemen's agreements" (Article XIX of GATT and Section IX of the proposed Code) but with somewhat looser standards. The program of the International Energy Agency, on the other hand, is intended to serve both the interests of national security (exempted from GATT under Article XXI and hence also from the Code) and to combat the restrictive trade actions on oil taken by the OPEC countries.

The illustrative text below would, in effect, recognize the continuing validity of the textile and oil arrangements while making explicit the non-interference of the Code with a member's GATT obligations to a non-member.

It would also, in paragraph 2, provide for periodic reporting to GATT and for consultations with contracting parties not members of the Code, particularly on development trade problems.

Illustrative Text

1. Nothing in this Code shall prevent any member:
   (a) from fulfilling its obligations under GATT to a contracting party to GATT which is not a member of the Code;
   (b) from applying exceptional measures relating to the international trade in textiles which conform to the requirements of the Geneva Arrangement Regarding International Trade in Textiles of December 20, 1973; or
   (c) from applying measures relating to the trade in oil or other energy

products necessary to implement the program or decisions of the International Energy Agency.

2. At the direction of the Executive Committee, the Director shall prepare and make available to the CONTRACTING PARTIES to GATT an annual report on the operation of the Code. The Executive Committee shall establish a Consultative Group of not more than five Executives or Alternates, which shall stand ready to meet and discuss from time to time with representatives of contracting parties not members of the Code, particularly in relation to the trade problems of developing contracting parties as they may bear on the operation of the Code, and to transmit the results of such discussions to the Executive Committee.

SECTION XII
Enforcement

Commentary

GATT's early and promising efforts to develop workmanlike, disinterested methods for interpreting obligations and settling disputes in the field of commercial disputes appear to have come to a standstill some time ago. One of the major criticisms of GATT today is that it is failing to provide effective machinery for handling disputes and enforcing obligations. The decline of GATT's effectiveness in this respect partly reflects its expansion to global membership coupled with the existence and broadening of a double standard of trade obligations under GATT: a fairly rigorous one for the industrialized countries and a very relaxed one for the less developed countries. Since GATT incorporates the one-country-one-vote system, it is not surprising that major trading nations have been increasingly reluctant to rely on GATT judgments for the interpretation and enforcement of trade commitments among themselves.

But some part of the difficulty lies in the text of GATT itself—particularly in the "nullification and impairment" provisions of Article XXIII. GATT's textual deficiencies for dealing with the enforcement problem might be summarized as follows:

1. Breaches of the GATT, whether in the form of outright violations of GATT obligations or actions which frustrate the obligations may be subject to redress (a) only upon the initiative of an affected contracting party, as a result of a complaint, (b) on grounds that a

51

benefit, presumably demonstrable, has been denied, and (c) after a written bilateral approach has been made to the offending contracting party. The GATT as such (acting, for example, on the advice of the Director-General) cannot on its own motion initiate such action even though the integrity of the multilateral rules might be involved.

2. A country adversely affected by a damaging trade action by another, even though it may be an outright violation of GATT, cannot retaliate unless the CONTRACTING PARTIES to GATT authorize it to do so, in advance, in "serious" circumstances.

3. There is no way in which the GATT organization can be required to act upon and discharge any matter referred to it. The result can be, and often is, frustration.

4. A failure to attain "any objective" of GATT (including, for example, full employment or raising standards of living) as a result of "the existence of any situation" can be treated under a literal reading of the text of GATT like an outright violation or a positive action which frustrates an obligation; except that in this case the matter may go directly to GATT without first proceeding bilaterally. This possible construction of the clause, although never in fact used, has been criticized by a GATT Working Party. It is clearly wrong in principle and should not be preserved in the Code.

5. No explicit provision is made for assistance from panels of disinterested persons. In the past, expert panels have been used in GATT on occasion and this device ought to be encouraged and broadened to include non-governmental persons as a means of introducing more objectivity.

The illustrative text shown below is designed to remedy, as among Code members, the defects of GATT's Article XXIII by setting up a new and different procedure for interpreting and enforcing the obligations of the Code. It should be noted that while the proposed illustrative text does not require bilateral efforts to settle differences before the Code machinery may be brought into action, it may be assumed that bilateral talks before international machinery is brought into play will continue to be the normal practice; but the institutions of the Code could, where desirable, initiate action themselves.

Illustrative Text

In their commercial relations with each other members shall apply the following provisions in lieu of Article XXIII of GATT:

1. The Executive Committee shall investigate expeditiously cases in which there is reason to believe that a member (a) may be failing to fulfill its obligations under this Code or (b) may have taken action which is depriving another member of economic benefits reasonably anticipated to result from the fulfill-

ment of such obligations or is lessening significantly the value of such benefits. Such investigations may be initiated by the Executive Committee or
undertaken at the request of any member. The Executive Committee may
determine to postpone or not to undertake an investigation requested by a
member, if the Committee considers that the material submitted by the requesting member in support of an investigation is inadequate to warrant the
investigation. The Executive Committee shall publish the reasons for its determination not to undertake an investigation requested of it.

2. The Executive Committee shall make and publish its findings and decision resulting from investigations pursuant to paragraph 1, above:

    (a) whether there is a failure to fulfill obligations by a member under this
        Code; or

    (b) whether an action has been taken by a member which deprives another
        member of economic benefits that could be reasonably anticipated from
        the fulfillment of Code obligations or lessens significantly the value
        of such benefits; or

    (c) that the evidence is inconclusive, that no decision is warranted and that
        the matter may not be considered again in the absence of additional
        evidence adequate to warrant another investigation.

Each member concerned shall provide the Executive Committee with all information available to it which is relevant to the Executive Committee's investigations. If a member fails to provide information that is available to it, the
Executive Committee shall proceed to a decision and may assume that the
information withheld is adverse to the member withholding it.

3. If the Executive Committee shall not have made its decision on a request
made by a member under paragraph 1, above, within 120 days from the receipt
of the request, the member that made the request shall then be free to suspend
or modify provisionally the application to the member or members referred to
in the first sentence of paragraph 2, above, of obligations under this Code
having equivalent effect to those involved in the investigation. The Executive
Committee may, however, after it has completed its investigation, determine
that such provisional action be changed or withdrawn.

4. If the Executive Committee decides that a member has (a) failed to fulfill
its Code obligations or (b) taken action which deprives another member of
economic benefits that could be reasonably anticipated from the fulfillment of
Code obligations or lessens significantly the value of such benefits, the
member or members adversely affected may suspend or modify the application to the first-named member of equivalent Code obligations, subject to the
right of the Executive Committee to define, at the time its decision is reached,
the limits or duration of any suspension or modification.

5. The Executive Committee as well as the Trade Council may appoint and
determine the terms of reference of panels of independent and disinterested
persons to assist them in carrying out the provisions of this Section.

6. Decisions of the Executive Committee under this Section may be appealed by any member to the Trade Council within 90 days from the date of
the interpretation or decision which shall, however, remain in force pending
action by the Trade Council. Action by the Trade Council shall be final.

SECTION XIII
Exceptions

Commentary

GATT was brought into force in 1947, and remains in force today, under a "Protocol of Provisional Application." One aspect of this 28-year old "provisional" arrangement, which is of special importance to the United States, is that most of GATT's trade rules apply only "to the fullest extent not inconsistent with [the then] existing legislation." In other words, the United States was not required to change domestic legislation that might otherwise conflict with one or more of GATT's trade rules. A good example is the rule in paragraph 6(a) of Article VI of GATT that, "No contracting party shall levy any . . . countervailing duty on the importation of any product . . . unless it determines that the effect of the . . . subsidization . . . is such as to cause or threaten . . . injury to an established domestic industry." This provision was in contradiction to the U.S. countervailing duty law which called for the mandatory imposition of countervailing duties to offset foreign subsidies or bounties even though no U.S. industry might be injured by the subsidy. The "grandfather clause" of the Protocol of Provisional Application quoted above, by limiting the U.S. commitment to those matters within the power of the Executive, avoided the conflict between GATT law and U.S. domestic law.

The "grandfather clause" of the Protocol of Provisional Application has come in for much criticism, not just because it is a loophole for various exceptions, but, perhaps more importantly, because it conceals the nature and scope of these exceptions. The countervailing duty case is only one of several loopholes applicable to the United States. Similar loopholes are applicable to other countries.

One of the legal concepts of the proposed Code of Trade Liberalization, set out in paragraph 1 of the Final Provision, is that every member shall, when signing the Code, certify that it has taken all legal steps to carry out its obligations under the Code. In other words the "grandfather clause" technique of covering up exceptions would be abandoned. If exceptions are to be made available to specific members for specific practices, they should be spelled out as part of the Code itself so that all governments, including their legislative arms, and the public in general, would be fully informed of their nature and extent. This is the purpose of the illustrative text below.

If the United States and other Code members should alter domestic legislation to conform with all of the Code trade rules, including all those incorporated from GATT, then of course neither a "grandfather clause" nor an exceptions provision would be required in the proposed Code.

Illustrative Text

> Any exceptions from the obligations of a member under Sections I through XI of this Code shall be limited to the specific trade measures and practices of that member listed and described in the Exceptions Annex to this Code, which is made an integral part thereof.
>
> The Trade Council shall review periodically the exceptions provided for in this Section with a view to their elimination or curtailment as soon as practicable. The first such review shall be conducted not later than five years after the entry into force of the Code.

SECTION XIV
Annexes for Prospective Signatories

Commentary

Several sections of the proposed Code would permit specified exceptions from Code rules if these exceptions are spelled out in annexes negotiated simultaneously with the Code itself:

— waivers previously granted by GATT which it is desired to continue (paragraph 3 of Section I);

— tariffs on specified products for each member which would not be subject to the general tariff reduction rules (paragraph 4 of Section II);

— an existing interim agreement for a customs union or free trade area which does not fully qualify under the rules (paragraph 1 of Section V);

— specific agricultural products subject to various domestic support programs (paragraph 1 of Part A of Section VI); and

— the various trade measures and practices which have just been referred to in the commentary above on exceptions (Section XIII).

Since the original members negotiating the Code will have provided these various exceptions applicable to themselves, they must be prepared to accord the same consideration to new members which come along after the Code has been concluded. The illustrative text below is designed to accomplish this by authorizing the Trade Council to approve—in effect to negotiate—exceptions for a prospective signatory. No attempt has been made to suggest texts for specific Annexes to the Code.

Illustrative Text
    A prospective signatory may submit to the Trade Council annexes on its behalf which conform to the terms of paragraph 3 of Section I, paragraph 4 of Section II, paragraph 1 of Section V, paragraph I of Part A of Section VI, or Section XIII. Upon approval by the Trade Council Annexes so submitted shall be incorporated in this Code as an integral part thereof at the time of signature of the Code by the prospective signatory.

SECTION XV
Institutional Provisions

Commentary

Most of the illustrative text relating to the institutions of the Code explains itself. Some general observations may, however, be in order.

1. It is not the intention that the arrangements for administering the Code and furthering its objectives should take the form of another independent international agency, with its separate bureaucracy and prerogatives, along the lines of the specialized agencies of the United Nations. Instead, the objective is that institutional arrangements for the Code should be within an already established international organization. The preferred organization for this purpose would be GATT, on whose provisions most of the Code is based. But to create a Code administration within GATT would require the consent of not less than a majority of all the GATT members—that is 40-plus votes out of a total of 80-plus—most of which are developing countries that could not be expected to belong to the Code themselves at any early stage. Since approval of the requisite GATT majority cannot, therefore, be safely assumed, the illustrative text below would simply authorize the Trade Council of the Code to make arrangements for bringing the institutions of the Code, including all its staff and budget, "within an appropriate established international organization." If a majority of the GATT members should by chance reject the idea of a smaller Code group within GATT, the Trade Council would be in a position to arrange for bringing the Code staff and budget within the OECD, as was done in 1974 with the International Energy Agency.

56

The original membership of the Code, as envisaged in the illustrative text, would all be members of the OECD and would account for 18 of the 24 OECD members, the others being developing countries which presumably would not attempt to exercise a veto. In any case, an effort should be made to develop the closest possible relationships between the Code and GATT. For this reason provision is made in the illustrative text of the Code for the participation of the Director-General of GATT in the discussions of the Code's Trade Council and Executive Committee. Also, the Trade Council would be authorized to enter into an agreement with GATT (if the Code is not within GATT) as well as with other international bodies of a governmental character. Finally, provision has already been made (see Section XI), for a consultative group of Code members to receive views from GATT contracting parties which are not Code members. Because the various organs, and the budget, of the Code are meant to be established within an existing organization, no provision has been made for the usual "privileges and immunities" accorded international institutions and their staff.

2. The institutional arrangements envisaged for the Code would rely heavily on representation by those who have responsibility for the making of national policies (or, in the case of the European Community, of Community policies). Thus, the Executive Committee of the Code would consist of representatives having senior responsibilities for the formulation of trade policies in the various capitals, and the Trade Council (to meet at least once yearly) would consist of members at the cabinet level ("Ministerial Representatives"). The reason for this is simple: the post-war experience with international economic institutions has shown, almost invariably, that better results are achieved when those who are responsible for making and executing national policies meet together to thrash out and settle their differences than when they rely solely upon communications between their proxies. This does not mean that permanent representatives, ambassadors or other resident delegates based at the headquarters of institutions play no significant role. They do, but it is more to help to focus important issues and to prepare well for their international discussion than to serve as the customary vehicle for their resolution. Most of the achievements of the OECD, and indeed of GATT, bear this out; and even the International Monetary Fund has now found it desirable to supplement the work of its permanent and highly competent Executive Directors with meetings of a new 20-member Council composed of policy-makers from the various capitals. The illustrative text of the proposed Code would not dispense with permanent repre-

sentatives but would provide for them through the use of alternates to the principal members ("Executives") of the Executive Committee. If the Code is administered within GATT these alternates could be the local representatives designated by Code members to serve on GATT's Geneva-based Council. If the Code is brought within the OECD the alternates could be persons in the permanent OECD delegations in Paris.

3. The Director of the Code is envisaged as a person who, in addition to management of the staff, should be able to exercise a degree of leadership in furthering the objectives of the Code. For this reason it is proposed that the Director serve as Chairman of the Executive Committee and that he be accorded the right to initiate proposals for the consideration of the Committee.

4. The illustrative text for the proposed Code would abandon the one-country-one-vote system of GATT and incorporate the principle of weighted voting. The one-country-one vote principle presents serious practical difficulties if the intention is to accord to an international economic agency the authority necessary to make of it an effective decision-making body. As was remarked earlier, major trading nations have been increasingly reluctant to rely on decisions in GATT reached by majority vote in which a country with $50 *million* of foreign trade has the same vote as a country with $50 *billion* of trade.

Under the illustrative formula shown for the proposed Code, voting weights would be assigned to members according to the size of their external merchandise trade, imports and exports, plus one-tenth of the total votes to be divided equally among the members. Since the trade rules of the Code are not intended to discriminate against the outside world, and since the Code is designed to be open to any country prepared to accept its terms, a member's trade with the whole world is included. Since trade within the European Community is internal trade, it would be excluded in the calculation of voting power.

For illustrative purposes the text shown below assumes that 10 developed countries (counting the European Community as one) would be original members of the Code. For these original members the initial voting power would be specified in the text. The Trade Council, however, would be authorized to recalculate the total number and distribution of votes from time to time to reflect changes in the volume and distribution of world trade. It might be noted that, according to the 1972 trade figures utilized in the illustrative text, there would be a ratio of 1:1.34 between the voting power of the

United States and that of the European Community—virtually the same as the ratio found in the International Monetary Fund if the votes of the Community members are aggregated. Additional commentary on voting power is contained in explanatory notes inserted below in the body of the illustrative text for the convenience of the reader.

5. The term "illustrative text" has been used throughout this document to remind the reader that serviceable alternative versions could have been formulated for the various provisions of the proposed Code. The reminder is particularly apt for those provisions of the illustrative text (paragraphs 5 and 6 of Part B of Section XV) which would prescribe specific voting majorities for certain of the wider powers of the Trade Council. Many variations are possible for dealing with the sensitive issue of qualified majorities; and no doubt any provisions of this nature which might emerge from the negotiating process would look different from those suggested here.

Illustrative Text

PART A
Organs of the Code

The organs to administer the Code shall consist of:
— The Trade Council
— The Executive Committee
— The Director and staff.

PART B
The Trade Council

1. All powers and responsibilities not specifically vested in another organ of the Code shall be vested in the Trade Council. The Council shall also have the power:
- (a) To make recommendations to any member on any matter relating to the functioning of the Code or in furtherance of its objectives.
- (b) To adopt codes, rules and other agreements supplemental to the provisions of the Code.
- (c) To suspend temporarily, in whole or in part, specific obligations of a member with respect to specific products or trade practices.
- (d) To provide for participation by non-members in the work of the institutions of the Code on matters of common concern.
- (e) To enter into arrangements with other international or supranational institutions, bodies and groups of a governmental character.
- (f) To establish, by regulation, procedures for the expression of views to the institutions of the Code by non-governmental groups and individuals.
- (g) To establish, by regulation, procedures to assure the confidentiality and rapid conclusion of consultations or discussions between a

member and any of the organs of the Code, or within an organ of the Code, in cases in which public knowledge of the consultations or discussions might give rise to speculative or preemptive movements in international trade, monetary or service transactions.

2. The Trade Council shall consist of a Ministerial Representative and an Alternate Representative appointed by each member. It shall select one of the Ministerial Representatives as Chairman.

3. The Trade Council shall meet annually and at such other times as it may determine. The Council shall by regulation establish procedures whereby its decisions and actions may be taken without requiring a meeting of the Council. The Council shall invite the Director-General to the CONTRACTING PARTIES to GATT to participate in meetings of the Council without vote, in accordance with regulations prescribed by the Council.

4. Unless specifically stated otherwise in the Code, the decisions and other actions of the Trade Council shall be agreed upon by a majority of the votes cast in accordance with the allotment of voting power stated in Part E of this Section, below.

5. The decisions and other actions of the Trade Council shall be binding upon all the members, except that:

(a) A decision or other action which imposes new obligations on members shall not apply to those members which vote against it unless the decision or action is taken by an affirmative vote of not less than 75 percent of the total voting power of all the members. If a member fails to carry out such a decision or action and does not exercise its right of withdrawal from the Code within a reasonable period, the Council may determine, by the same voting majority, that the Code ceases to apply in respect of that member.

(b) The Council may decide, by a majority of the total voting power of all the members, that a decision or action which imposes new obligations on members shall apply only to those members voting affirmatively on such decision or action.

6. Decisions of the Council which reduce the obligations of a member pursuant to paragraph 1(c) of this Part, and decisions pursuant to Section XIV of the Code, shall require the affirmative vote of a majority of the members which majority shall have not less than 60 percent of the total voting power of all the members.

7. The Trade Council may delegate to the Executive Committee authority to exercise any of its powers except the power to:

(a) Approve amendments to the Code.

(b) Approve formal agreements with other intergovernmental institutions.

(c) Decide appeals from the interpretations, decisions and other actions of the Executive Committee.

(d) Determine, pursuant to paragraph 5(a) of this part or paragraph 2 of Section XVIII, that the Code ceases to apply in respect of a member.

(e) Take decisions pursuant to Section XIV.

PART C
The Executive Committee

1. The Executive Committee shall be responsible for the general administration of the Code. It shall exercise all powers specifically assigned to it by other provisions of the Code or delegated to it by the Trade Council, and shall perform all functions required of it by the Council. It shall approve the annual budget of administrative expenses of the Code. It may appoint subcommittees or other subgroups, including panels of disinterested persons, to assist it in its work.

2. The Executive Committee shall consist of one Executive and one Alternate appointed by each member. Each Executive shall be a senior official having substantial responsibilities for the formulation of the international trade policies of the member appointing him. The Executive Committee shall meet as frequently as necessary for the conduct of its work. The Director-General to the CONTRACTING PARTIES to GATT shall be invited to participate in meetings of the Executive Committee, without vote, in accordance with regulations prescribed by the Committee.

3. Each Executive shall be entitled to cast the votes allotted to the appointing member in Part E of this Section. In the absence of the Executive the Alternate for the member may cast its votes. Decisions and other actions of the Executive Committee shall be agreed upon by a majority of the votes cast, except that paragraphs 5 and 6 of Part B of this Section shall also apply to voting in the Executive Committee.

PART D
The Director and Staff

1. The Director shall be appointed by the Executive Committee and shall remain in office for the period determined by the Committee. He shall be head of staff of the Code and shall perform such other functions as the Executive Committee shall prescribe. He shall have the right to initiate proposals for the consideration of the Committee.

2. The Director shall be Chairman of the Executive Committee, but shall have no vote except a deciding vote in case of an equal division. He may participate, without vote, in the meetings of the Trade Council.

3. The Trade Council shall take all necessary decisions to assure the functioning of the Director and staff and to provide for the financing of the organs of the Code. The Council, as soon as practicable, shall seek arrangements for bringing the organs and budget of the Code within the framework of an appropriate established international institution. Each member of the Code shall contribute to the annual expenses incurred by reason of the operation of the Code, as determined by the Executive Committee pursuant to paragraph 1 of Part C of this Section, in the proportion which its voting power bears to the total voting power of all the members.

PART E
Voting Power

1. When this Code enters into force, each member shall have the voting power specified in the table below. Thereafter, the voting power of members shall be reviewed periodically and determined by the Trade Council in accordance with the provisions of paragraphs 3 and 4 of this Part.

	Trade Votes	Basic Votes	Total Votes	(Percentage Distribution of Voting Power)*
Australia	11.4	4.4	15.8	(3.58)
Austria	8.9	4.4	13.3	(3.01)
Canada	39.1	4.4	43.5	(9.84)
European Community	142.8	4.4	147.2	(33.31)
Japan	48.5	4.4	52.9	(11.97)
New Zealand	3.2	4.4	7.6	(1.72)
Norway	7.4	4.4	11.8	(2.67)
Sweden	16.1	4.4	20.5	(4.64)
Switzerland	15.2	4.4	19.6	(4.44)
United States	105.3	4.4	109.7	(24.82)
Totals	397.9	44.0	441.9	(100.00)

*Explanatory notes to table shown above:

1. It is not intended that the column of percentages at the right, or these explanatory notes, would appear in any text of a Code as finally negotiated.

2. The trade figures used in calculating voting power are based on 1972 data compiled by the OECD and the U.S. Department of Commerce as summarized and published by the U.S. Department of State in its news release of August 1973. Imports on a c.i.f. basis were adjusted to f.o.b. according to the relationship between imports c.i.f. and imports f.o.b. shown for individual countries for 1972 in International Financial Statistics *of the International Monetary Fund.*

2. When the Code becomes effective for a member not listed in paragraph 1 of this Part, it shall be entitled, until the next determination of the voting power of the members, to: (1) the number of votes provided for in paragraph 3(a) of this Part calculated as if it were a member at the time of the last preceding calculation of voting power for the members; plus (2) a number of votes equal to the number of votes members were last individually allocated according to the column headed "Basic Votes" in paragraph 1 of this Part or, when the voting power indicated in that column has been superseded, according to paragraph 3(b) of this Part.

3. Except as otherwise provided in this Part, each member shall be entitled to voting power determined as follows:

(a) Ninety percent of the aggregate voting power of all members shall be calculated by allotting to each member one vote for each one billion United States dollars (equivalent) of its total external trade. For the purposes of this paragraph, the external trade of a member shall comprise its average annual exports plus its average annual imports during a period of three consecutive years, which years shall be the same for all members.

(b) Ten percent of the aggregate voting power of all members shall be divided among them in equal amounts.

4. The Trade Council shall determine the date when voting power shall be reviewed and when any revision in voting power shall become effective; the period that shall be deemed to be "the period of three consecutive years";

and, after consultation with the International Monetary Fund, the exchange rates to be utilized in determining the equivalent of United States dollars. The Trade Council may establish such supplementary rules and procedures as may be necessary for the calculation of voting power.

SECTION XVI
Interpretation

Commentary

No explicit provision is made for authoritative interpretations of GATT obligations by the GATT organization, i.e., the CONTRACTING PARTIES. It may be reasonably argued that this power is implicit in various provisions of GATT and, indeed, GATT has acted as though it were. For purposes of the Code, the power to interpret would be made explicit and would be vested in the Executive Committee with right of appeal to the Trade Council.

Illustrative Text

1. Any question of interpretation of the provisions of this Code arising between members shall be submitted to the Executive Committee for its decision.

2. Interpretations of the Executive Committee under this Section may be appealed by any member to the Trade Council within 90 days from the date of the interpretation which shall, however, remain in force pending action by the Trade Council. Action by the Trade Council shall be final.

SECTION XVII
Withdrawal

Commentary

If the institutions of the Code are to be effective they must be accorded certain powers to make binding decisions by votes of less than unanimity—for example, to interpret the Code's trade rules, to relax when necessary certain of its obligations, to adopt supplemental trade rules imposing new obligations and to amend the Code formally on a basis applicable to all members. These and similar responsibilities would be given to the Trade Council or the Executive Committee by various provisions elsewhere in the illustrative text. Nations may be more likely to accord responsibilities of this kind to an international institution, and the institution be more likely to use them with discretion, if an individual member can withdraw at any time it feels that its interests are no longer served by continued membership.

Illustrative Text

Any member may withdraw from the Code at any time effective upon receipt of written notice to the Director.

SECTION XVIII
Amendments

Commentary

The amendment procedure suggested is similar to that governing amendments to the International Monetary Fund Agreement except that amendments would not automatically apply to all members; the Trade Council would be required to specify that an amendment must apply to all, in which case a member rejecting it would have to withdraw. The withdrawal privilege could not be altered except by an amendment approved unanimously.

Illustrative Text

1. Amendments to the Code shall become effective upon approval by the Trade Council by an affirmative vote of a majority of the members with not less than 80 percent of the total voting power of all the members, but no amendment altering the right of withdrawal of a member under Section XVII shall be approved except upon an affirmative vote of all the members.

2. The Trade Council may provide, in an instrument of amendment, that the amendment shall apply to all the members and that a member failing to apply it may be required to withdraw from the Code.

FINAL PROVISION

Commentary

The only aspect of the "Final Provision" of the illustrative text that may deserve special comment is that it provides for members to certify at the time of signature that they have taken all legal steps necessary to enable them to fulfill their Code obligations. This is intended to avoid a repetition of the much-criticized "grandfather clause" situation regarding GATT discussed earlier in the commentary on Section XIII. The idea of a signature *after* national governments (and the European Community) have approved the Code is the reverse of the practice in many international agreements of signing first and ratifying, or accepting, later.

Illustrative Text

1. Each Government and the European Community, on whose behalf this Code is signed, shall at the time of its signature deposit with the Director-General to the CONTRACTING PARTIES to GATT an instrument stating that it has taken all legal steps necessary to enable it to carry out its obligations under this Code.

2. This Code shall enter into force for its signatories _____ days after it has been signed on behalf of the European Community, Japan and the United States, and for each other signatory named in paragraph 1 of Part E of Section XV thirty days after the day of its signature.

3. This Code shall be open for signature by any other government which is a contracting party to GATT and a member of the International Monetary Fund.

DISSENTING COMMENTS BY R. M. BRENNAN

The fundamental issue of whether or not international commodity arrangements are desirable, workable or avoidable is not discussed in the report. However, the language of the report, as it addresses the question of international commodity arrangements, by implication indicates the Atlantic Council's support of this concept. I believe such an endorsement is premature. As of this writing, for example, various agencies within the U.S. government are separately studying this problem. It would be unfortunate if these agencies should interpret these Atlantic Council statements as favoring such commodity arrangements, particularly if such an endorsement was not intended by the drafters of this report. Accordingly, I would like to disassociate myself from even an implied support of such international commodity arrangements.

It is not my position to categorically prejudge international commodity arrangements as unworkable or unacceptable. However, I am not comfortable that the acceptance of this concept has been analyzed to the extent warranted.

Although the market system has imperfections, it has proven to be the best long-term allocator of resources. The abandonment of the market system in favor of the cartel, commodity arrangement system is not a decision to be made in the absence of careful study and discussion. It is an essential policy decision, with important long range ramifications on the future of world trade and the role of the U.S. and U.S. corporations in that trading environment.

How an international commodity arrangement will actually function and work must be analyzed. For example, will buffer stocks be used, will a supranational agency move in and out of the market to control price levels, what will be the source of its funds, how will the U.S. direct (rationalize) the production of its producers, will it be necessary to amend U.S. antitrust laws and regulations, will the U.S. be willing to have its coal, timber or other resources exported to other nations, how would this impact on Project Independence, will Congressional approval be needed, will it be forthcoming? The Communist nations of the world control a large number of scarce resources—will they be part of an agreement? If not, will they be excluded from the markets of the world? If permitted to sell in the open market could these nations effectuate havoc in the commodity arrangement system by sporadic entries into the marketplace?

It is possible that the approach adopted at the Lomé convention might be a more workable, less complicated approach to the problem facing the developing countries. My purpose is not one of advocacy of one system over another—it is simply to highlight the complexity and importance of the issue and to call for careful analysis before even an indirect or implied support of international commodity arrangements is made.

If indeed, the policy decision is made that joining international commodity arrangements is in the best long-term interest of the U.S., then certainly the guidelines set forth in the report would be essential. Namely, that "both producing and consuming countries participate equitably in their negotiations and administration."

DISSENTING COMMENTS BY W. D. EBERLE

I strongly support the objectives which motivated the development of this proposed code: expanding trade and tightening trade rules while improving their enforcement. In principle, a code of this kind can be used to achieve these objectives. However, there are several aspects of this specific code that might take us farther away from these aims.

There is a great need to strengthen the guidelines governing trade and compliance within those guidelines. Such reform is necessary to preserve the progress we have made already and to give governments the confidence to move toward continued trade liberalization.

The multilateral negotiations (MTN) underway in Geneva have the potential to fulfill these needs. The MTN has a broad base of support: governments representing industrialized, semi-industrialized and developing countries are participating. The involvement of all countries in as many issues as possible is essential to progress in reform of the global trading system.

The proposed code could be useful as one tool. It could be utilized either as a method to strengthen GATT rules in a limited area beyond the issues taken up in the MTN or as a catalyst, should the progress of the negotiations be impeded for some reason.

When such a code is employed, there are several areas that should be modified. First, membership in the code should be open to all countries. However, I believe benefits of the code should be restricted to those countries assuming its obligations. To extend the benefits of agreements consummated under the code to all countries, whether or not they are members of the code eliminates any incentive to non-members to assume its obligations.

Secondly, the issues to be covered in such a code must be selected with care to encourage the continued constructive participation by the developing countries. There should be no attempt to isolate them by creating a "rich man's club" within GATT. Issues such as access to supplies, so important to both the developing and industrialized nations, must be pursued by all concerned countries.

Finally, I think that too much attention has been focused on the decision-making mechanism. Voting is desirable in the application of sanctions for actions contrary to GATT, but is not desirable in negotiating agreements. Nations seeking to agree on more rigorous obligations will find it more useful to rely on consensus decision-making.

Manipulation of procedural rules will not create the political will needed to do the job. Working together to establish agreements and guidelines is essential to the creation of an atmosphere of confidence within which countries will be willing to undertake the expanded obligations that an open trading system implies.

APPENDIX A

Illustrative Text of
Proposed Code of Trade Liberalization

ESTABLISHMENT PROVISION

The Governments and the Council of the European Community, on whose behalf this Code is signed, agree as follows:

1. A Code of Trade Liberalization (hereinafter called the "Code") is hereby established in furtherance of the objectives of the General Agreement on Tariffs and Trade (hereinafter called "GATT") and shall be carried out in accordance with the following provisions.

2. The term "members" means those on whose behalf this Code is signed and which are represented in the Trade Council and the Executive Committee under the provisions of Section XV of the Code.

3. Each member undertakes to collaborate with the organs of the Code to further the liberalization of international trade and to eliminate unfair international trade practices.

SECTION I
Application of GATT Trade Rules

1. Members of the Code undertake to apply in commercial relations among themselves Articles I through XVII and XIX through XXIV to GATT (together with Annex I and such other Annexes to GATT as are relevant for members and are still in force) in accordance with, and subject to, the other provisions of this Code. Wherever the term "contracting party" is used in GATT, it shall be understood for the purposes of the Code to mean a "member" of the Code; and wherever the term "CONTRACTING PARTIES" is used in GATT, it shall be understood to mean for the purposes of the Code the members of the Code acting through the Trade Council and Executive Committee as provided for in Section XV to the Code.

2. Articles XVIII, XXV through XXXV and Part IV of GATT shall not be construed to modify the rights and obligations of members established by the Code.

3. Waivers granted by the CONTRACTING PARTIES pursuant to Article XXV of GATT prior to the effective date of this Code shall not apply to the obligations described in paragraph 1, above, unless they are specifically listed in the Waivers Annex of this Code, which is made an integral part thereof.

71

SECTION II
Reduction of Tariffs

1. An objective of the Code shall be to achieve, in time, the elimination of the customs tariffs of the members. As a first step toward the achievement of this objective, members shall apply the following provisions of this Section.

2. Except as provided in paragraph 3 of this Section, products imported into the territory of any member which are the products of any other member shall, upon their importation, be exempt from most-favored-nation ordinary customs duties in excess of the duties described below, and shall be exempt from all other duties and charges of any kind imposed on or in connection with importation in excess of those imposed on January 1, 1975, or those directly and mandatorily required to be imposed thereafter by legislation in force in the importing territory on that date:

   (a) No rate of duty existing on January 1, 1975, including zero rates of duty, shall be increased.
   (b) If the rate of duty existing on January 1, 1975, is not more than 5 percent *ad valorem*, it shall be eliminated over a period of not more than two years.
   (c) If the rate of duty existing on January 1, 1975, is more than 5 percent *ad valorem* but not more than 10 percent *ad valorem*, it shall be reduced to 5 percent *ad valorem* over a period of not more than two years.
   (d) If the rate of duty existing on January 1, 1975, is more than 10 percent *ad valorem* but not more than 20 percent *ad valorem*, it shall be reduced to 8 percent *ad valorem* over a period of not more than 4 years.
   (e) If the rate of duty existing on January 1, 1975, is more than 20 percent *ad valorem*, it shall be reduced to not more than 40 percent of the rate existing on January 1, 1975, over a period of not more than 10 years.
   (f) No member shall be required by the provisions of subparagraphs (c) or (d) of this paragraph to reduce the rate of duty on any product to a rate below 40 percent of the rate existing on January 1, 1975.

3. The maximum rates of duty provided for in paragraph 2, above, shall be applied in accordance with the detailed rules and timetable described in Tariff Annex No. 1 of this Code, which is made an integral part thereof.

4. The exceptions to paragraph 2, above, shall be those specified in Tariff Annexes Nos. 2 through _____, which shall also state the maximum tariff rates applicable to the named products in the territories of the members concerned. These Annexes are made an integral part of this Code.

5. The principles of paragraphs 2, 3, 4 and 5 of Article 11 of GATT shall also apply to the import tariff obligations of members under this Code.

6. The Trade Council may, by a majority of the votes cast, authorize a member to increase the rate of duty on any product above the maximum rate provided for by paragraph 2 of this Section, above, if the majority of votes cast includes the affirmative votes of all members having a substantial interest as suppliers of the product concerned.

7. If a developed contracting party to GATT fails to adhere to the Code within a reasonable period after its entry into force, or if a member of the Code ceases to be a member, the Trade Council may authorize any member to suspend the application of the provisions of this Section to products principally supplied by that contracting party or former member. The Trade Council may make regulations for carrying out the provisions of this paragraph.

72

SECTION III
Access to Supplies and Technology

1. No prohibition or restriction on the export or sale for export of any product applied by any member pursuant to paragraph 2(a) of Article XI or to paragraphs (g) or (i) of Article XX of GATT shall be applied to the export or sale for export of any product destined for the territory of any other member, nor shall any tax, duty or other charge be newly imposed or, if now imposed, increased by any member on the export or sale for export of any product destined for the territory of any other member, except after consultation through the Trade Council. Any such prohibition, restriction, tax, duty or charge shall be administered consistently with the objective of assuring the equitable sharing of scarce supplies between essential domestic and foreign requirements, taking into account the shares prevailing in a prior representative period and any special factors affecting the trade in the product concerned. Any member applying a trade measure pursuant to this paragraph shall remove it as soon as the circumstances giving rise to its application shall have ceased to exist.

2. Each member affirms that any measure it may adopt pursuant to paragraph (j) of Article XX of GATT as being essential to the acquisition or distribution of a product in general or in local short supply shall be consistent with the principle of the equitable international sharing of the supply of that product. If any member proposes to adopt any measure, or proposes to enter into an international agreement, to assure to itself access to a product in short supply, it shall first consult through the Trade Council with respect to the consistency of the proposed measure or agreement with the above principle.

3. The members affirm that concerted intergovernmental measures to restrict production or trade in any product for the purpose of limiting its international supply or maintaining or increasing its international price must take the form of an intergovernmental commodity agreement providing for equitable representation by consuming and producing countries alike in the negotiation and administration of the agreement. Accordingly, members agree that in their commercial relations with each other they will apply the following provision in lieu of paragraph (h) of Article XX of GATT:

"(h) undertaken in pursuance of obligations under any intergovernmental commodity agreement which provides for equitable participation by both consuming and producing countries;"

4. In the event of a continuing shortage, however caused, of the international supply of a non-renewable resource, the members shall, upon the request of any of them, consult through the Trade Council, GATT, the Organization for Economic Cooperation and Development, or any other appropriate international institution, regarding the best means of increasing the supply or reducing the demand of the non-renewable resource, including measures designed to increase or share the existing supply, develop alternative or substitute sources of supply, alter patterns of consumption or improve technology. Any measures adopted pursuant to this paragraph and having the approval of the Trade Council may be applied by any member notwithstanding other provisions of this Code.

5. No member shall prevent, limit or tax the export on a commercial basis of

73

privately-owned technology to the territory of another member. This paragraph shall not prevent any member from imposing a charge on the export of such technology in order to recover the costs of governmental research and development if the charge is no higher than that made for the same technology when sold domestically on a commercial basis. This paragraph shall not prevent measures applied in respect of technology for the moral, health or enforcement purposes described in paragraphs (a), (b) and (d) of Article XX of GATT or those taken for the essential security interests described in Article XXI of GATT.

SECTION IV
The Use of Quantitative Restrictions

1. No member shall require licenses or permits as a condition for the importation of any product of the territory of any other member or for the exportation of any product destined for the territory of any other member except for the purpose of enforcing prohibitions or restrictions authorized under the provisions of this Code.

2. Members shall, in their commercial relations with each other, adhere to the provisions of Section VI of the Code in lieu of the provisions of paragraph 2(c) of Article XI of GATT insofar as that paragraph relates to agricultural products.

SECTION V
Equality of Trade Treatment

1. No member shall maintain or enter into an interim agreement leading to a customs union or free-trade area without the prior approval of the Trade Council. The Trade Council shall grant such approval if it finds that the proposed interim agreement meets the conditions and requirements set forth in paragraphs 5(a), 5(b), and 5(c) of Article XXIV of GATT. (Note: any exception for a specific existing arrangement from the requirements of this paragraph would have to be agreed upon before signature of the Code and recorded in an Annex to it.)

2. The Trade Council may adopt regulations for the observance and administration of the provisions of paragraph 1, above, which paragraph, together with any regulations adopted by the Trade Council, shall supersede the provisions of paragraph 7 of Article XXIV of GATT in commercial relations among members.

3. No member which is party to an interim agreement for a customs union or free-trade or other preferential or discriminatory arrangement with a country which claims in respect of that member privileges comparable to those

accorded to developing countries under Article XVIII or Part IV of the GATT shall invoke its legal claims under such interim agreement or other preferential or discriminatory arrangement, nor shall it apply or threaten measures of trade retaliation or other economic sanction, to prevent the developing country from according full equality of trade treatment, as defined in Article I, and in other provisions of GATT, to the trade of any other member.

4. This Section shall not prevent any member from extending, without reciprocity, preferences to the trade of any developing country or to that of any territory, not a part of its customs territory, for which it has responsibility.

SECTION VI
Agriculture

Part A
Applicability of Code Trade Provisions
to Certain Agricultural Products

1. Agricultural products shall be exempt from the provisions of Section II of the Code and of Article II of GATT, as incorporated in the Code, insofar as these provisions limit charges on imports other than ordinary customs duties, and Article XI of GATT as incorporated in the Code, but shall be subject to the provisions of Section VI of the Code, if:

(a) Such agricultural products are or become subject to internal governmental measures or programs that operate to support domestic agricultural prices or incomes, to control domestic production, acreage or marketing, or to manage domestic surpluses or supplies, which internal governmental measures or programs would be seriously endangered by the failure to apply trade measures inconsistent with the provisions of the Code and GATT referred to in paragraph 1 above; and

(b) Such agricultural products are specified in the Agricultural Annex to the Code, either on the effective date of the Code or by later approval of the Trade Council; and subject to such conditions as may be stated in the Annex.

2. Agricultural products of the members which are not subject to Section VI of the Code shall be subject to all of the other provisions of the Code.

3. Notwithstanding the provisions of paragraph 1, above, if a prohibition, restriction, tax, duty or other charge is applied by any member on the export or sale for export of any agricultural product (whether or not subject to the provisions of Section VI of the Code) destined for the territory of any other member, the principles of paragraph 1 of Section III of the Code shall apply.

Part B
Supplemental Agricultural Agreements

1. Adequate intergovernmental assurances to further the stability and growth of international trade in the agricultural products specified in the

Agricultural Annex are an essential part of the understandings among members embodied in the Code. Accordingly, members undertake to provide such assurances through the conclusion and periodic renewal of Supplemental Agricultural Agreements for products specified in the Agricultural Annex. The objectives of such agreements shall include the achievement of mutually advantageous understandings regarding:

(a) the adjustment of the internal measures or programs referred to in paragraph 1(a) of Part A of this Section (or alternatively commitments with respect to conventional barriers to international trade in the products subject to such measures or programs) in such a way as to enable the gradual widening of opportunities for international trade in the agricultural products concerned;

(b) measures to assure security of access to supplies for importing countries and security of access to markets for exporting countries, including the establishment, where appropriate, of internationally coordinated stockpiles to help in meeting shortages and stabilizing international prices; and

(c) the encouragement of structural adjustments in agriculture to improve and stabilize the income of farmers while enabling production and sales to meet the requirements of expanding consumption at reasonable prices.

2. Supplemental Agricultural Agreements may include participation by governments not members of the Code and may provide for the administration and operation of such agreements separately from the institutions of the Code in accordance with procedural and voting arrangements agreed upon by the participants in such agreements.

3. Members of the Code participating in a Supplemental Agricultural Agreement or engaged in negotiations for the conclusion of such an agreement shall, upon the request of any member of the Code, or upon the request of the Trade Council, consult with the Trade Council regarding the effect of the agreement or proposed agreement on the trade of members in the light of the objectives required of such agreements by the provisions of paragraph 1, above, of Part B of this Section.

SECTION VII
Trade Measures Relating to the International Monetary System

In their commercial relations with each other, members shall apply the following provisions in lieu of Articles XII, XIV, and XV of GATT:

1. Nothing in this Code shall prevent any member from applying import restrictions or other trade measures for the purpose of safeguarding its balance of payments and reserve position if such action:

(a) has been approved by the International Monetary Fund pursuant to the Articles of Agreement of the Fund or pursuant to an arrangement between the Fund and the members of the Code, or is otherwise authorized by the Articles of the Agreement of the Fund; or

(b) has been approved by the Trade Council.

2. The Trade Council shall be empowered to make decisions in accordance with clause (b) of paragraph 1 of this Section only if it finds that clause (a) is of no effect because the International Monetary Fund is not empowered to approve the application of trade measures and the Articles of Agreement of the Fund do not otherwise authorize the application of trade measures. If the Trade Council so finds, it shall seek an agreement with the Fund respecting participation by the Fund whenever the Trade Council is considering the approval of trade measures pursuant to clause (b).

3. With respect to trade measures applied by a member pursuant to clause (b) of paragraph 1 of this Section, the Trade Council may specify a schedule of consultations between the Trade Council and the member, requirements for the progressive relaxation of such measures, a date for the expiration of its approval, and any other conditions it considers to be appropriate. With respect to trade measures applied pursuant to clause (a), the Trade Council may require consultations between the Trade Council and the member concerning the administration of such measures, and, pursuant to arrangements with the International Monetary Fund, may participate in consultations between the Fund and the member.

4. Within 30 days after the Trade Council convenes, each member shall notify the Trade Council of the trade measures it is applying for the purpose of safeguarding its balance of payments and reserve position. As soon as possible, the Trade Council shall make a determination pursuant to paragraph 2 of this Section whether it may proceed in accordance with clause (b) of paragraph 1 of this Section and, if so, shall decide whether the trade measures so notified shall be approved. Pending a decision pursuant to paragraph 1, trade measures so notified shall not be deemed inconsistent with the provisions of the Code.

5. A member applying import restrictions under paragraph 1 of this Section shall administer them in accordance with the principles of paragraph 3(c) of Article XII of GATT.

6. No member shall invoke the provisions of Article II or Article XVI of GATT to prevent the application by another member of import surcharges or export subsidies applied pursuant to paragraph 1 of this Section, and each member shall take such legal steps as may be open to it to modify any of its international obligations to non-members which might prevent such application.

7. The Trade Council shall seek cooperation with the International Monetary Fund to the end that the Trade Council and the Fund may pursue coordinated policies, within their respective jurisdictions, in furtherance of their common objectives.

SECTION VIII
Subsidies, Countervailing Duties, Dumping and Antidumping Practices

1. Members shall apply the following provisions in lieu of paragraph 4 of Article XVI of GATT:
(Note: This would list the new, detailed definitions of prohibited export subsidies which it is hoped will emerge from the Geneva Multilateral Trade Negotiations, at least insofar as developed countries are concerned.)

2. Members shall, upon the request of the Trade Council, provide it with all information available to them regarding specific governmental actions or practices of a member which the Council believes may constitute a subsidy in terms of any provision of Article XVI of GATT as incorporated in the Code. The Council may, for the purposes of the Code, define specific actions or practices of a member, or kinds or classes of actions or practices of members generally, as constituting such subsidies.

3. Any member considering the imposition of a countervailing duty on the importation of a product of another member shall, not less than 120 days prior to the imposition of such duty, notify the Trade Council and shall promptly consult with such other member and, upon request of the Trade Council, with the Council. In any case in which the Trade Council determines that the product is being exported with benefit of an export subsidy prohibited by the terms of paragraph 1 of this Section, the member considering the imposition of a countervailing duty on such product shall not be required to make the determination regarding material injury to domestic industry referred to in paragraph 6(a) of Article VI of GATT.

4. In their commercial relations with each other, members shall apply the antidumping provisions of GATT as interpreted and elaborated by Articles 1 through 12 of the Agreement on Implementation of Article VI of the General Agreement on Tariffs and Trade of June 30, 1967.

SECTION IX
Safeguard Provisions

Members shall observe the following provisions supplementary to those of Article XIX of GATT incorporated in the Code pursuant to paragraph 1 of Section 1 of the Code:

1. No member shall enter into or facilitate an intergovernmental or other international voluntary or other arrangement for the application of trade measures which limits import competition, whether by export restraints or otherwise, with its domestic producers unless such arrangement shall have been approved by the Trade Council in accordance with the provisions of paragraphs 3 and 4 below.

2. The Trade Council shall, not later than two years after the entry into force of the Code, review, in the light of the requirements for arrangements

set forth in paragraphs 3 and 4 below, arrangements existing on the date of the entry into force of the Code. If the Council disapproves such an existing arrangement, the arrangement shall be terminated forthwith.

3. The Trade Council shall not approve an arrangement proposed to be concluded after the entry into force of the Code, unless it is convinced that the arrangement is warranted by unusual circumstances affecting the trade of the importing member, including:

(a) a large increase in imports has occurred over a short period of time affecting adversely an industry which is of substantial importance to the economy of the country desiring to restrict imports; and

(b) such industry has not been capable of adjusting to such import competition during that period of time; and

(c) the member desiring to restrict imports has initiated a process of adopting appropriate domestic adjustment measures.

4. Such an arrangement proposed to be concluded after the entry into force of the Code shall not be approved by the Trade Council unless it is satisfied that:

(a) the initial levels of permitted imports are not less than those which occurred during a recent representative period, and upward adjustments in the levels of permitted imports are provided for periodically during the time the arrangements are in force, in appropriate proportion to anticipated or actual increases in domestic consumption; and

(b) appropriate compensation or withdrawal of concessions, as the case may be, is afforded or made available to members adversely affected thereby, unless in special circumstances the Trade Council, by a two-thirds majority of the votes cast, finds that such compensation or withdrawal is not appropriate;

(c) import-limiting measures are applied in respect to all members which are substantial suppliers of the product concerned on a most-favored-nation basis, unless in special circumstances the Trade Council finds, by a two-thirds majority of the votes cast, that the general application of such measures is not appropriate;

(d) the duration of any arrangement is limited to three years, with any renewal subject to approval by the Trade Council as if it were an original arrangement.

5. During the existence of any arrangement approved by the Trade Council, under paragraphs 1 or 2, above, the Trade Council shall hold annual consultations for the purpose of determining the extent to which the arrangement meets the conditions set forth in paragraphs 3 and 4, above.

6. Any Code member may at any time request the Trade Council to hold consultations concerning the application of an arrangement which the Trade Council has approved, in which event the Council shall convene a consultation within thirty days of the request. The Council may withdraw its approval of the arrangement following any consultation pursuant to this paragraph if it finds that the conditions of paragraphs 3 and 4 are not being met, in which event the arrangement shall no longer be of any force and effect.

SECTION X
Nontariff Barriers: Procedures for the Future

1. The members affirm their common interest in achieving the curtailment or elimination of existing policies and practices, other than ordinary customs duties, which introduce inequities and distortions into the international trading system to the benefit of domestic producers or consumers and to the disadvantage of foreign producers or consumers, and in preventing the adoption of new policies and practices of this kind in the future. They undertake to collaborate with the organs of the Code in furtherance of these objectives.

2. Subject to the provisions of paragraph 3 of this Section, any member considering the adoption of a measure which would apply to a product of another member, whether or not it would also apply to the like domestic product, or which would apply to the export of a domestic product, shall notify the Trade Council prior to making such measure effective and shall, if requested by another member, or by the Trade Council, consult with the other member or the Council; as the case may be, regarding (a) the consistency of the proposed measure with the obligations under the Code of the member considering the adoption of the measure and (b) whether or not the measure is consistent with such obligations, any adverse effect it may have on the trade of the other member. This paragraph shall enter into force upon the expiration of one year after the entry into force of the Code.

3. The Trade Council may, by regulation approved by a majority of the votes cast, establish rules for the application of paragraph 2 of this Section, including rules for waiving the requirement for prior notification and consultation in emergency circumstances.

4. The Trade Council shall, within two years after the entry into force of the Code, establish a system for the periodic, intensive review of the policies and practices of each member, whether or not such policies or practices are consistent with the member's obligations under the Code, which affect the conditions of international competition. Members shall provide the Trade Council with all information necessary for the effective conduct of such reviews. In the light of such reviews the Trade Council may, in accordance with the provisions of Section XV of the Code, make recommendations to members, adopt supplemental codes or take other appropriate action in furtherance of the objectives stated in paragraph 1 of this Section.

SECTION XI
Relationship of Code to Certain Other Multilateral Trade Arrangements

1. Nothing in this Code shall prevent any member:
(a) from fulfilling its obligations under GATT to a contracting party to GATT which is not a member of the Code;

    (b) from applying exceptional measures relating to the international trade in textiles which conform to the requirements of the Geneva Arrangement Regarding International Trade in Textiles of December 20, 1973; or

    (c) from applying measures relating to the trade in oil or other energy products necessary to implement the program or decisions of the International Energy Agency.

2. At the direction of the Executive Committee, the Director shall prepare and make available to the CONTRACTING PARTIES to GATT an annual report on the operation of the Code. The Executive Committee shall establish a Consultative Group of not more than five Executives or Alternates, which shall stand ready to meet and discuss from time to time with representatives of contracting parties not members of the Code, particularly in relation to the trade problems of developing contracting parties as they may bear on the operation of the Code, and to transmit the results of such discussions to the Executive Committee.

SECTION XII
Enforcement

In their commercial relations with each other members shall apply the following provisions in lieu of Article XXIII of GATT:

1. The Executive Committee shall investigate expeditiously cases in which there is reason to believe that a member (a) may be failing to fulfill its obligations under this Code or (b) may have taken action which is depriving another member of economic benefits reasonably anticipated to result from the fulfillment of such obligations or is lessening significantly the value of such benefits. Such investigations may be initiated by the Executive Committee or undertaken at the request of any member. The Executive Committee may determine to postpone or not to undertake an investigation requested by a member, if the Committee considers that the material submitted by the requesting member in support of an investigation is inadequate to warrant the investigation. The Executive Committee shall publish the reasons for its determination not to undertake an investigation requested of it.

2. The Executive Committee shall make and publish its findings and decision resulting from investigations pursuant to paragraph 1, above:

    (a) whether there is a failure to fulfill obligations by a member under this Code; or

    (b) whether an action has been taken by a member which deprives another member of economic benefits that could be reasonably anticipated from the fulfillment of Code obligations or lessens significantly the value of such benefits; or

    (c) that the evidence is inconclusive, that no decision is warranted and that the matter may not be considered again in the absence of additional evidence adequate to warrant another investigation.

Each member concerned shall provide the Executive Committee with all information available to it which is relevant to the Executive Committee's investigations. If a member fails to provide information that is available to it, the Executive Committee shall proceed to a decision and may assume that the information withheld is adverse to the member withholding it.

3. If the Executive Committee shall not have made its decision on a request made by a member under paragraph 1, above, within 120 days from the receipt of the request, the member that made the request shall then be free to suspend or modify provisionally the application to the member or members referred to in the first sentence of paragraph 2, above, of obligations under this Code having equivalent effect to those involved in the investigation. The Executive Committee may, however, after it has completed its investigation, determine that such provisional action be changed or withdrawn.

4. If the Executive Committee decides that a member has (a) failed to fulfill its Code obligations or (b) taken action which deprives another member of economic benefits that could be reasonably anticipated from the fulfillment of Code obligations or lessens significantly the value of such benefits, the member or members adversely affected may suspend or modify the application to the first-named member of equivalent Code obligations, subject to the right of the Executive Committee to define, at the time its decision is reached, the limits or duration of any suspension or modification.

5. The Executive Committee as well as the Trade Council may appoint and determine the terms of reference of panels of independent and disinterested persons to assist them in carrying out the provisions of this Section.

6. Decisions of the Executive Committee under this Section may be appealed by any member to the Trade Council within 90 days from the date of the interpretation or decision which shall, however, remain in force pending action by the Trade Council. Action by the Trade Council shall be final.

SECTION XIII
Exceptions

Any exceptions from the obligations of a member under Sections I through XI of this Code shall be limited to the specific trade measures and practices of that member listed and described in the Exceptions Annex to this Code, which is made an integral part thereof.

The Trade Council shall review periodically the exceptions provided for in this Section with a view to their elimination or curtailment as soon as practicable. The first such review shall be conducted not later than five years after the entry into force of the Code.

SECTION XIV
Annexes for Prospective Signatories

A prospective signatory may submit to the Trade Council annexes on its behalf which conform to the terms of paragraph 3 of Section I, paragraph 4 of Section II, paragraph 1 of Section V, paragraph I of Part A of Section VI, or Section XIII. Upon approval by the Trade Council Annexes so submitted shall be incorporated in this Code as an integral part thereof at the time of signature of the Code by the prospective signatory.

SECTION XV
Institutional Provisions

PART A
Organs of the Code

The organs to administer the Code shall consist of:
— The Trade Council
— The Executive Committee
— The Director and staff.

PART B
The Trade Council

1. All powers and responsibilities not specifically vested in another organ of the Code shall be vested in the Trade Council. The Council shall also have the power:

(a) To make recommendations to any member on any matter relating to the functioning of the Code or in furtherance of its objectives.

(b) To adopt codes, rules and other agreements supplemental to the provisions of the Code.

(c) To suspend temporarily, in whole or in part, specific obligations of a member with respect to specific products or trade practices.

(d) To provide for participation by non-members in the work of the institutions of the Code on matters of common concern.

(e) To enter into arrangements with other international or supranational institutions, bodies and groups of a governmental character.

(f) To establish, by regulation, procedures for the expression of views to the institutions of the Code by non-governmental groups and individuals.

(g) To establish, by regulation, procedures to assure the confidentiality and rapid conclusion of consultations or discussions between a member and any of the organs of the Code, or within an organ of the Code, in cases in which public knowledge of the consultations or discussions might give rise to speculative or preemptive movements in international trade, monetary or service transactions.

2. The Trade Council shall consist of a Ministerial Representative and an Alternate Representative appointed by each member. It shall select one of the Ministerial Representatives as Chairman.

3. The Trade Council shall meet annually and at such other times as it may determine. The Council shall by regulation establish procedures whereby its decisions and actions may be taken without requiring a meeting of the Council. The Council shall invite the Director-General to the CONTRACTING PARTIES to GATT to participate in meetings of the Council without vote, in accordance with regulations prescribed by the Council.

4. Unless specifically stated otherwise in the Code, the decisions and other actions of the Trade Council shall be agreed upon by a majority of the votes cast in accordance with the allotment of voting power stated in Part E of this Section, below.

5. The decisions and other actions of the Trade Council shall be binding upon all the members, except that:

(a) A decision or other action which imposes new obligations on members shall not apply to those members which vote against it unless the decision or action is taken by an affirmative vote of not less than 75 percent of the total voting power of all the members. If a member fails to carry out such a decision or action and does not exercise its right of withdrawal from the Code within a reasonable period, the Council may determine, by the same voting majority, that the Code ceases to apply in respect of that member.

(b) The Council may decide, by a majority of the total voting power of all the members, that a decision or action which imposes new obligations on members shall apply only to those members voting affirmatively on such decision or action.

6. Decisions of the Council which reduce the obligations of a member pursuant to paragraph 1(c) of this Part, and decisions pursuant to Section XIV of the Code, shall require the affirmative vote of a majority of the members which majority shall have not less than 60 percent of the total voting power of all the members.

7. The Trade Council may delegate to the Executive Committee authority to exercise any of its powers except the power to:

(a) Approve amendments to the Code.

(b) Approve formal agreements with other intergovernmental institutions.

(c) Decide appeals from the interpretations, decisions and other actions of the Executive Committee.

(d) Determine, pursuant to paragraph 5(a) of this part or paragraph 2 of Section XVIII, that the Code ceases to apply in respect of a member.

(e) Take decisions pursuant to Section XIV.

PART C
The Executive Committee

1. The Executive Committee shall be responsible for the general administration of the Code. It shall exercise all powers specifically assigned to it by other provisions of the Code or delegated to it by the Trade Council, and shall perform all functions required of it by the Council. It shall approve the annual budget of administrative expenses of the Code. It may appoint subcommittees or other subgroups, including panels of disinterested persons, to assist it in its work.

2. The Executive Committee shall consist of one Executive and one Alternate appointed by each member. Each Executive shall be a senior official having substantial responsibilities for the formulation of the international trade policies of the member appointing him. The Executive Committee shall meet as frequently as necessary for the conduct of its work. The Director-General to the CONTRACTING PARTIES to GATT shall be invited to participate in meetings of the Executive Committee, without vote, in accordance with regulations prescribed by the Committee.

3. Each Executive shall be entitled to cast the votes allotted to the appointing member in Part E of this Section. In the absence of the Executive the Alternate for the member may cast its votes. Decisions and other actions of the Executive Committee shall be agreed upon by a majority of the votes cast, except that paragraphs 5 and 6 of Part B of this Section shall also apply to voting in the Executive Committee.

PART D
The Director and Staff

1. The Director shall be appointed by the Executive Committee and shall remain in office for the period determined by the Committee. He shall be head of staff of the Code and shall perform such other functions as the Executive Committee shall prescribe. He shall have the right to initiate proposals for the consideration of the Committee.

2. The Director shall be Chairman of the Executive Committee, but shall have no vote except a deciding vote in case of an equal division. He may participate, without vote, in the meetings of the Trade Council.

3. The Trade Council shall take all necessary decisions to assure the functioning of the Director and staff and to provide for the financing of the organs of the Code. The Council, as soon as practicable, shall seek arrangements for bringing the organs and budget of the Code within the framework of an appropriate established international institution. Each member of the Code shall contribute to the annual expenses incurred by reason of the operation of the Code, as determined by the Executive Committee pursuant to paragraph 1 of Part C of this Section, in the proportion which its voting power bears to the total voting power of all the members.

PART E
Voting Power

1. When this Code enters into force, each member shall have the voting power specified in the table below. Thereafter, the voting power of members shall be reviewed periodically and determined by the Trade Council in accordance with the provisions of paragraphs 3 and 4 of this Part.

	Trade Votes	Basic Votes	Total Votes	(Percentage Distribution of Voting Power)*
Australia	11.4	4.4	15.8	(3.58)
Austria	8.9	4.4	13.3	(3.01)
Canada	39.1	4.4	43.5	(9.84)
European Community	142.8	4.4	147.2	(33.31)
Japan	48.5	4.4	52.9	(11.97)
New Zealand	3.2	4.4	7.6	(1.72)
Norway	7.4	4.4	11.8	(2.67)
Sweden	16.1	4.4	20.5	(4.64)
Switzerland	15.2	4.4	19.6	(4.44)
United States	105.3	4.4	109.7	(24.82)
Totals	397.9	44.0	441.9	(100.00)

Explanatory notes to table shown above:

1. It is not intended that the column of percentages at the right, or these explanatory notes, would appear in any text of a Code as finally negotiated.

2. The trade figures used in calculating voting power are based on 1972 data compiled by the OECD and the U.S. Department of Commerce as summarized and published by the U.S. Department of State in its news release of August 1973. Imports on a c.i.f. basis were adjusted to f.o.b. according to the relationship between imports c.i.f. and imports f.o.b. shown for individual countries for 1972 in International Financial Statistics *of the International Monetary Fund.*

2. When the Code becomes effective for a member not listed in paragraph 1 of this Part, it shall be entitled, until the next determination of the voting power of the members, to: (1) the number of votes provided for in paragraph 3(a) of this Part calculated as if it were a member at the time of the last preceding calculation of voting power for the members; plus (2) a number of votes equal to the number of votes members were last individually allocated according to the column headed "Basic Votes" in paragraph 1 of this Part or, when the voting power indicated in that column has been superseded, according to paragraph 3(b) of this Part.

3. Except as otherwise provided in this Part, each member shall be entitled to voting power determined as follows:

(a) Ninety percent of the aggregate voting power of all members shall be calculated by allotting to each member one vote for each one billion United States dollars (equivalent) of its total external trade. For the purposes of this paragraph, the external trade of a member shall comprise its average annual exports plus its average annual imports during a period of three consecutive years, which years shall be the same for all members.

(b) Ten percent of the aggregate voting power of all members shall be divided among them in equal amounts.

4. The Trade Council shall determine the date when voting power shall be reviewed and when any revision in voting power shall become effective; the period that shall be deemed to be "the period of three consecutive years"; and, after consultation with the International Monetary Fund, the exchange rates to be utilized in determining the equivalent of United States dollars. The Trade Council may establish such supplementary rules and procedures as may be necessary for the calculation of voting power.

SECTION XVI
Interpretation

1. Any question of interpretation of the provisions of this Code arising between members shall be submitted to the Executive Committee for its decision.

2. Interpretations of the Executive Committee under this Section may be appealed by any member to the Trade Council within 90 days from the date of the interpretation which shall, however, remain in force pending action by the Trade Council. Action by the Trade Council shall be final.

SECTION XVII
Withdrawal

Any member may withdraw from the Code at any time effective upon receipt of written notice to the Director.

SECTION XVIII
Amendments

1. Amendments to the Code shall become effective upon approval by the Trade Council by an affirmative vote of a majority of the members with not less than 80 percent of the total voting power of all the members, but no amendment altering the right of withdrawal of a member under Section XVII shall be approved except upon an affirmative vote of all the members.

2. The Trade Council may provide, in an instrument of amendment, that the amendment shall apply to all the members and that a member failing to apply it may be required to withdraw from the Code.

FINAL PROVISION

1. Each Government and the European Community, on whose behalf this Code is signed, shall at the time of its signature deposit with the Director-General to the CONTRACTING PARTIES to GATT an instrument stating that it has taken all legal steps necessary to enable it to carry out its obligations under this Code.

2. This Code shall enter into force for its signatories _____ days after it has been signed on behalf of the European Community, Japan and the United States, and for each other signatory named in paragraph 1 of Part E of Section XV thirty days after the day of its signature.

3. This Code shall be open for signature by any other government which is a contracting party to GATT and a member of the International Monetary Fund.

APPENDIX B

A Note on the Use of Support Margins *(Montants de Soutien)* in Negotiations for Supplemental Agricultural Agreements

One of the problems in agricultural trade negotiations has been the difficulty of comparing the degree of protection afforded by various techniques of support such as tariffs, variable levies, import quotas, mixing regulations, production subsidies, and export subsidies. The cleanest way of dealing with this problem would be to use fixed tariffs as the only permissible technique of protection and to ban the use of all other devices. But this approach is not negotiable. The Europeans and Japanese oppose it on the ground that it would expose their domestic producers and consumers to excessive fluctuations in world markets. The United States also uses nontariff devices to protect its agriculture. The experience of the last three years reinforces the lesson of earlier history that fixed tariffs will not work for trade in certain basic agricultural products. Institutional inertia is another factor to be reckoned with. Techniques of government intervention are entrenched in existing legislation and institutions and are, therefore probably more difficult to change than the *levels* of support and protection. For example, it is certain that there would be strong opposition in the United States to any proposal to scrap the present system of dairy support prices and import quotas and to rely on tariffs as the sole means of protecting the dairy industry.

An alternative approach would be to permit countries to continue the existing techniques of support and protection provided their overall protective effect is gradually reduced. This approach would permit the European Community to continue to offset year-to-year fluctuations in world prices through the use of variable levies; but the average level of these levies would be gradually reduced. This could be brought about by keeping increases in EC domestic prices below the rate of increase in world prices. In the U.S. the rate of increase of dairy support prices could be similarly slowed down *pari passu* with a gradual increase in import quotas. This could be accomplished without abandoning the existing system of support and protection, although it would require a change in the legislative provision which sets the floor price at 75% of "parity."

While the negotiability of this approach remains to be tested, it is generally consistent with proposals made by the EC during the Kennedy Round.[1] It would be responsive to mounting pressures within the EC (particularly in the UK and Germany) to restrain the rise in food prices and to limit the costs of the Common Agricultural Policy (CAP). It may be significant that the European and Japanese participants in the tripartite conference on agricultural trade held in the Brookings Institution in September 1973 endorsed a 50% reduction of the general level of agricultural protection over ten years on this basis (with the proviso that reductions in real farm prices should not exceed 3% in any one year).[2]

Measuring the Level of Protection

A prerequisite of this approach is the reduction of the various measures of support and protection to a common denominator which could be used to compare their protective effect and to serve as a basis for determining the equivalence of reciprocal concessions.

The EC during the Kennedy Round proposed that the *montant de soutien* (margin of support) be used for this purpose. The *MdS* essentially represents the difference between domestic producer prices and world prices. Domestic producer prices would include not only the price received by producers on the domestic market but also any product-specific subsidies such as price support (deficiency or supplemental) payments (but not general subsidies such as governmental research and extension services, input subsidies, social welfare-type payments, adjustment assistance, etc.). The world price would be represented by a "reference price" which would reflect production costs in efficient exporting countries. Export prices and domestic producer prices would be adjusted for transportation costs to major ports of export and import, respectively.

Table 1 shows support margins for wheat, corn and cheese in the EC and the U.S., for the period 1968-70 and projections for "1976/ 77." The latter should not be interpreted as forecasts for that particular year but rather, as a rough indication of the "normal" price relationships that may be expected on the assumption that world grain production catches up with demand, grain stocks are restored to normal levels, and world inflation levels off. The projections show:

---

[1] *Although the EC offered no more than a binding, for 3 years, of existing support margins, the technique lends itself to a gradual reduction of levels of protection.*

[2] Toward the Integration of World Agriculture, *Brookings Institution, October 1973.*

Table 1
Level of Protection
(MdS = % by which domestic price[a] exceeds world price[b];
prices in dollars per metric ton).

	EC			US		
	Domestic price	World price	*MdS*	Domestic price	World price	*MdS*
1968/70						
Wheat [c]	116	62	87%	88	57	54%
Corn	94	59	60%	67	55	22%
Cheese [d]	1250	566	120%	1300	566	130%
Projected **"1976/77"** [e]						
Wheat [c]	242	110	120%	100	100	0%
Corn	196	100	96%	90	90	0%
Cheese [d]	2200	1000	120%	2280	1000	128%

a *Domestic price = support price adjusted for transportation costs to the point of import (Rotterdam) or export (Gulf ports). For the U.S., support prices for 1968-1970 include value of price support payments (marketing certificates and export subsidies for wheat, direct payments and diversion payments for corn, and storage subsidies under the resale program).*

b *World price = f.o.b. for exporting countries, c.i.f. for importing countries*

c *Wheat = U.S. No. 2 Hard Winter, 13.5% protein. European wheat adjusted for quality differential.*

d *Cheese = New Zealand cheddar and nearest EC and U.S. equivalents.*

e *Based on the following assumptions:*

(i) EC grain target prices in 1976/77 will be 18% higher than in 1974-75 (7% higher than in 1975/76);

(ii) Supported domestic prices for dairy products in the EC and U.S. will be 75% above 1968-70.

(iii) The currency conversion factor, used to convert EC threshold prices to current dollars, will be approximately equal to its 1974/75 level ($1.50).

(iv) World grain prices will revert to their 1971-72 relationship with costs of production in the U.S. and other major exporting countries, as measured by the U.S. index of prices paid for inputs. The index of prices paid, now about 150% of 1971-72, will have risen to 170% by 1976/77.

(v) U.S. producer returns for grains (adjusted for transportation costs to ports) will be equal to export prices since under present legislation, no direct payments will be made to producers so long as prices prevailing in the open (domestic and world) market exceed the target prices.

(vi) World prices of cheese will be 80% above 1968-70.

— EC grain support prices exceeding world prices by greater margins than in 1968/70;
— U.S. producer prices for grain at world market levels because market prices at the levels projected would be high enough not to trigger deficiency payments provided under present U.S. legislation;
— Dairy support margins in the EC and U.S. still over twice the world market level, despite the projected increase in world prices.

How the Approach Would Work

Use of the *MdS* approach would require agreement on the following points:

(1) *Initial position.* The negotiators might agree that the figures for "1976/77" in Table 1 are an accurate reflection of the new "normal" situation, or they may wish to make certain adjustments for what they consider abnormalities. In general, determination of prices received by producers should pose no serious problems. Determination of reference prices representing the anticipated long-term equilibrium level of world prices (i.e., the average prices that would clear the world market over the next 3 years or so in the absence of subsidies) does, of course, involve an element of judgment. The recent upheaval in world agricultural prices makes it unusually difficult to gauge future equilibrium price levels. Prior to the price surge, a moving average of prices during the preceding three years might have served as a guide. In the impending trade negotiations, the price experience of 1972-75 will have to be largely disregarded. Hopefully, by the time the negotiations are wound up (in 1978?), world agricultural prices will have returned to their normal relation with production costs in efficient exporting countries, i.e., to levels in the neighborhood of those projected for "1976/77" in Table 1.

It is important to keep in mind that the reference price has only one function: to serve as a base for estimating margins of support; it is *not* a trading price to be forced upon the market. Furthermore, as an estimate of the underlying long-term world equilibrium price, it is subject to revision on the basis of actual world prices in subsequent years (see (3) below). Thus any errors in the initial determination of the margin of support are also subject to subsequent correction.

(2) *Schedule of Reduction of MdS.* The negotiators will have to agree on the extent and phasing of reductions—for example, 50% over 10 years, in 5 linear installments. Assuming that the EC's *MdS* on wheat has been determined to be 120% as in Table 1, each biennial

91

reduction in the *MdS* would be one-fifth of 60% or 12%. The domestic support price would thus be reduced by $66 per ton, from $242 per ton in 1976/77 to $176 per ton in 1986/87. The first reduction, applicable in 1977/78 and 1978/79 would be one-fifth of $66 or $13.20, giving a support price of $228.80. In the second two-year period, the support price would drop to $215.60.

(3) *Review of Reference Prices*. Reference prices could be reviewed every two years by a standing committee of the participants in the Supplemental Agricultural Agreements, along with other aspects of the agreement. For example, if the course of actual world prices in 1977/78-1978/79 suggests an equilibrium price for wheat of $120 instead of $110 per ton for the following 2-year period, the maximum support prices in the schedule would be raised from $215.60 to $235.20, giving an *MdS* of 96% as called for in the schedule.

(4) *Adjustment for Inflation*. In the event of continuing world-wide inflation of production costs, world prices as well as national support prices would rise, more or less *pari passu*. It may be argued that the procedure suggested under (3) above would cause excessive delays in the adjustment of support levels to take account of this. An alternative approach would be continuous adjustments of both reference and support prices on the basis of a world index of production costs which in turn, would be subject to review every two years.

Should a participant experiencing more than average inflation of production costs be permitted to make a further upward adjustment in its support levels? If so, it would follow that a participant experiencing less than average inflation would have to make downward adjustments. On the whole, it would seem preferable to rely on exchange rate adjustments to correct differences in rates of inflation. A country experiencing more than average inflation will sooner or later devalue its currency; this will raise the national currency equivalent of the support price, thus relieving the situation of its agricultural producers.

(5) *Review of Performance*. The biennial review should provide opportunities to correct any inequities arising from the application of the agreement. For example, if the world price dropped more than foreseen when setting the reference price and as a result, the actual margin of support failed to decline, there may be a *prima facie* case for reducing the reference price for the next period. But it is also possible that the scheduled reduction of the *MdS* actually takes place but is impaired by some other governmental action, not included in the definition of "support." While the *MdS* approach is designed to minimize this risk, it should nevertheless be covered by an effective review procedure.

PART
II
TEXT OF THE
GENERAL AGREEMENT ON
TARIFFS AND TRADE, 1969

PREFACE

This volume contains the text of the General Agreement as in force on 1 March 1969. The text incorporates the amendments to the General Agreement which have become effective since November 1958, when Volume III was published. The principal change is the addition of Articles XXXVI to XXXVIII following the entry into force of the Protocol Amending the General Agreement to Introduce a Part IV on Trade and Development which has been accepted by nearly all contracting parties. A guide to the legal sources of the provisions of the Agreement is provided in an Appendix. An Analytical Index (second revision), containing notes on the drafting, interpretation and application of the Articles of the Agreement, was published by the secretariat in February 1966.

The General Agreement is applied " provisionally " by all contracting parties. The original contracting parties, and also those former territories of Belgium, France, the Netherlands and the United Kingdom which, after attaining independence, acceded to the General Agreement under Article XXVI: 5 (c), apply the GATT under the Protocol of Provisional Application, the text of which is reproduced in this volume. Chile applies the General Agreement under a Special Protocol of September 1948. The contracting parties which have acceded since 1948 apply the General Agreement under their respective Protocols of Accession.

For the convenience of the reader, **asterisks** mark the portions of the text which should be read in conjunction with notes and supplementary provisions in Annex I to the Agreement. In accordance with Article XXXIV, Annexes A to I are an integral part of the Agreement. The Schedules of tariff concessions annexed to the General Agreement (not here reproduced) are also, in accordance with Article II: 7, an integral part of the Agreement.

By the Decision of 23 March 1965, the CONTRACTING PARTIES changed the title of the head of the GATT secretariat from " Executive Secretary " to " Director-General ". However, in the absence of an amendment to the General Agreement to take account of this change, the title " Executive Secretary " has been retained in the text of Articles XVIII: 12 (e), XXIII: 2, and XXVI: 4, 5 and 6. The Decision of 23 March 1965 provides that the duties and powers conferred upon the Executive Secretary by the General Agreement " shall be exercised by the person holding the position of Director-General, who shall, for this purpose, also hold the position of Executive Secretary ".

TABLE OF CONTENTS

THE GENERAL AGREEMENT ON TARIFFS AND TRADE

The Governments of the COMMONWEALTH OF AUSTRALIA, the KINGDOM OF BELGIUM, the UNITED STATES OF BRAZIL, BURMA, CANADA, CEYLON, the REPUBLIC OF CHILE, the REPUBLIC OF CHINA, the REPUBLIC OF CUBA, the CZECHOSLOVAK REPUBLIC, the FRENCH REPUBLIC, INDIA, LEBANON, the GRAND-DUCHY OF LUXEMBURG, the KINGDOM OF THE NETHERLANDS, NEW ZEALAND, the KINGDOM OF NORWAY, PAKISTAN, SOUTHERN RHODESIA, SYRIA, the UNION OF SOUTH AFRICA, the UNITED KINGDOM OF GREAT BRITAIN AND NORTHERN IRELAND, and the UNITED STATES OF AMERICA:

Recognizing that their relations in the field of trade and economic endeavour should be conducted with a view to raising standards of living, ensuring full employment and a large and steadily growing volume of real income and effective demand, developing the full use of the resources of the world and expanding the production and exchange of goods,

Being desirous of contributing to these objectives by entering into reciprocal and mutually advantageous arrangements directed to the substantial reduction of tariffs and other barriers to trade and to the elimination of discriminatory treatment in international commerce,

Have through their Representatives agreed as follows:

PART I

Article I

General Most-Favoured-Nation Treatment

1.   With respect to customs duties and charges of any kind imposed on or in connection with importation or exportation or imposed on the international transfer of payments for imports or exports, and with respect to the method of levying such duties and charges, and with respect to all rules and formalities in connection with importation and exportation, and with respect to all matters referred to in paragraphs 2 and 4 of Article III, * any advantage, favour, privilege or immunity granted by any contracting party to any product originating in or destined for any other country shall be accorded immediately and unconditionally to the like product originating in or destined for the territories of all other contracting parties.

2.   The provisions of paragraph 1 of this Article shall not require the elimination of any preferences in respect of import duties or charges which do not exceed the levels provided for in paragraph 4 of this Article and which fall within the following descriptions:

   (*a*) Preferences in force exclusively between two or more of the terri- tories listed in Annex A, subject to the conditions set forth therein;

   (*b*) Preferences in force exclusively between two or more territories which on July 1, 1939, were connected by common sovereignty or relations of protection or suzerainty and which are listed in Annexes B, C and D, subject to the conditions set forth therein;

   (*c*) Preferences in force exclusively between the United States of America and the Republic of Cuba;

   (*d*) Preferences in force exclusively between neighbouring countries listed in Annexes E and F.

3.   The provisions of paragraph 1 shall not apply to preferences between the countries formerly a part of the Ottoman Empire and detached from it on July 24, 1923, provided such preferences are approved under para- graph 5 † of Article XXV, which shall be applied in this respect in the light of paragraph 1 of Article XXIX.

---

† The authentic text erroneously reads " sub-paragraph 5 (*a*) ".

4. The margin of preference * on any product in respect of which a preference is permitted under paragraph 2 of this Article but is not specifically set forth as a maximum margin of preference in the appropriate Schedule annexed to this Agreement shall not exceed:

(a) in respect of duties or charges on any product described in such Schedule, the difference between the most-favoured-nation and preferential rates provided for therein; if no preferential rate is provided for, the preferential rate shall for the purposes of this paragraph be taken to be that in force on April 10, 1947, and, if no most-favoured-nation rate is provided for, the margin shall not exceed the difference between the most-favoured-nation and preferential rates existing on April 10, 1947;

(b) in respect of duties or charges on any product not described in the appropriate Schedule, the difference between the most-favoured-nation and preferential rates existing on April 10, 1947.

In the case of the contracting parties named in Annex G, the date of April 10, 1947, referred to in sub-paragraphs (a) and (b) of this paragraph shall be replaced by the respective dates set forth in that Annex.

Article II

Schedules of Concessions

1. (a) Each contracting party shall accord to the commerce of the other contracting parties treatment no less favourable than that provided for in the appropriate Part of the appropriate Schedule annexed to this Agreement.

(b) The products described in Part I of the Schedule relating to any contracting party, which are the products of territories of other contracting parties, shall, on their importation into the territory to which the Schedule relates, and subject to the terms, conditions or qualifications set forth in that Schedule, be exempt from ordinary customs duties in excess of those set forth and provided for therein. Such products shall also be exempt from all other duties or charges of any kind imposed on or in connection with importation in excess of those imposed on the date of this Agreement or those directly and mandatorily required to be imposed thereafter by legislation in force in the importing territory on that date.

(c) The products described in Part II of the Schedule relating to any contracting party which are the products of territories entitled under Article I to receive preferential treatment upon importation into the territory to which the Schedule relates shall, on their importation into such territory, and subject to the terms, conditions or qualifications set forth in that Schedule, be exempt from ordinary customs duties in excess of those set forth and provided for in Part II of that Schedule. Such products shall also be exempt from all other duties or charges of any kind imposed on or in connection with importation in excess of those imposed on the date of this Agreement or those directly and mandatorily required to be imposed thereafter by legislation in force in the importing territory on that date. Nothing in this Article shall prevent any contracting party from maintaining its requirements existing on the date of this Agreement as to the eligibility of goods for entry at preferential rates of duty.

2. Nothing in this Article shall prevent any contracting party from imposing at any time on the importation of any product:

(*a*) a charge equivalent to an internal tax imposed consistently with the provisions of paragraph 2 of Article III * in respect of the like domestic product or in respect of an article from which the imported product has been manufactured or produced in whole or in part;

(*b*) any anti-dumping or countervailing duty applied consistently with the provisions of Article VI;*

(*c*) fees or other charges commensurate with the cost of services rendered.

3. No contracting party shall alter its method of determining dutiable value or of converting currencies so as to impair the value of any of the concessions provided for in the appropriate Schedule annexed to this Agreement.

4. If any contracting party establishes, maintains or authorizes, formally or in effect, a monopoly of the importation of any product described in the appropriate Schedule annexed to this Agreement, such monopoly shall not, except as provided for in that Schedule or as otherwise agreed between the parties which initially negotiated the concession, operate so as to afford protection on the average in excess of the amount of protection provided for in that Schedule. The provisions of this paragraph shall not limit the use by contracting parties of any form of assistance to domestic producers permitted by other provisions of this Agreement.*

5. If any contracting party considers that a product is not receiving from another contracting party the treatment which the first contracting party believes to have been contemplated by a concession provided for in the appropriate Schedule annexed to this Agreement, it shall bring the matter directly to the attention of the other contracting party. If the latter agrees that the treatment contemplated was that claimed by the first contracting party, but declares that such treatment cannot be accorded because a court or other proper authority has ruled to the effect that the product involved

cannot be classified under the tariff laws of such contracting party so as to permit the treatment contemplated in this Agreement, the two contracting parties, together with any other contracting parties substantially interested, shall enter promptly into further negotiations with a view to a compensatory adjustment of the matter.

6. (*a*) The specific duties and charges included in the Schedules relating to contracting parties members of the International Monetary Fund, and margins of preference in specific duties and charges maintained by such contracting parties, are expressed in the appropriate currency at the par value accepted or provisionally recognized by the Fund at the date of this Agreement. Accordingly, in case this par value is reduced consistently with the Articles of Agreement of the International Monetary Fund by more than twenty per centum, such specific duties and charges and margins of preference may be adjusted to take account of such reduction; *Provided* that the CONTRACTING PARTIES (*i.e.*, the contracting parties acting jointly as provided for in Article XXV) concur that such adjustments will not impair the value of the concessions provided for in the appropriate Schedule or elsewhere in this Agreement, due account being taken of all factors which may influence the need for, or urgency of, such adjustments.

(*b*) Similar provisions shall apply to any contracting party not a member of the Fund, as from the date on which such contracting party becomes a member of the Fund or enters into a special exchange agreement in pursuance of Article XV.

7. The Schedules annexed to this Agreement are hereby made an integral part of Part I of this Agreement.

PART II

Article III *

National Treatment on Internal Taxation and Regulation

1. The contracting parties recognize that internal taxes and other internal charges, and laws, regulations and requirements affecting the internal sale, offering for sale, purchase, transportation, distribution or use of products, and internal quantitative regulations requiring the mixture, processing or use of products in specified amounts or proportions, should not be applied to imported or domestic products so as to afford protection to domestic production.*

2. The products of the territory of any contracting party imported into the territory of any other contracting party shall not be subject, directly or indirectly, to internal taxes or other internal charges of any kind in excess of those applied, directly or indirectly, to like domestic products. Moreover, no contracting party shall otherwise apply internal taxes or other internal charges to imported or domestic products in a manner contrary to the principles set forth in paragraph 1.*

3. With respect to any existing internal tax which is inconsistent with the provisions of paragraph 2, but which is specifically authorized under a trade agreement, in force on April 10, 1947, in which the import duty on the taxed product is bound against increase, the contracting party imposing the tax shall be free to postpone the application of the provisions of paragraph 2 to such tax until such time as it can obtain release from the obligations of such trade agreement in order to permit the increase of such duty to the extent necessary to compensate for the elimination of the protective element of the tax.

4. The products of the territory of any contracting party imported into the territory of any other contracting party shall be accorded treatment no less favourable than that accorded to like products of national origin in respect of all laws, regulations and requirements affecting their internal sale, offering for sale, purchase, transportation, distribution or use. The provisions of this paragraph shall not prevent the application of differential internal transportation charges which are based exclusively on the economic operation of the means of transport and not on the nationality of the product.

5. No contracting party shall establish or maintain any internal quantitative regulation relating to the mixture, processing or use of products in specified amounts or proportions which requires, directly or indirectly, that any specified amount or proportion of any product which is the subject of the regulation must be supplied from domestic sources. Moreover, no contracting party shall otherwise apply internal quantitative regulations in a manner contrary to the principles set forth in paragraph 1.*

6. The provisions of paragraph 5 shall not apply to any internal quantitative regulation in force in the territory of any contracting party on July 1, 1939, April 10, 1947, or March 24, 1948, at the option of that contracting party; *Provided* that any such regulation which is contrary to the provisions of paragraph 5 shall not be modified to the detriment of imports and shall be treated as a customs duty for the purpose of negotiation.

7. No internal quantitative regulation relating to the mixture, processing or use of products in specified amounts or proportions shall be applied in such a manner as to allocate any such amount or proportion among external sources of supply.

8. (*a*) The provisions of this Article shall not apply to laws, regulations or requirements governing the procurement by governmental agencies of products purchased for governmental purposes and not with a view to commercial resale or with a view to use in the production of goods for commercial sale.

(*b*) The provisions of this Article shall not prevent the payment of subsidies exclusively to domestic producers, including payments to domestic producers derived from the proceeds of internal taxes or charges applied consistently with the provisions of this Article and subsidies effected through governmental purchases of domestic products.

9. The contracting parties recognize that internal maximum price control measures, even though conforming to the other provisions of this Article, can have effects prejudicial to the interests of contracting parties supplying imported products. Accordingly, contracting parties applying such measures shall take account of the interests of exporting contracting parties with a view to avoiding to the fullest practicable extent such prejudicial effects.

10. The provisions of this Article shall not prevent any contracting party from establishing or maintaining internal quantitative regulations relating to exposed cinematograph films and meeting the requirements of Article IV.

Article IV

Special Provisions relating to Cinematograph Films

If any contracting party establishes or maintains internal quantitative regulations relating to exposed cinematograph films, such regulations shall take the form of screen quotas which shall conform to the following requirements:

(a) Screen quotas may require the exhibition of cinematograph films of national origin during a specified minimum proportion of the total screen time actually utilized, over a specified period of not less than one year, in the commercial exhibition of all films of whatever origin, and shall be computed on the basis of screen time per theatre per year or the equivalent thereof;

(b) With the exception of screen time reserved for films of national origin under a screen quota, screen time including that released by administrative action from screen time reserved for films of national origin, shall not be allocated formally or in effect among sources of supply;

(c) Notwithstanding the provisions of sub-paragraph (b) of this Article, any contracting party may maintain screen quotas conforming to the requirements of sub-paragraph (a) of this Article which reserve a minimum proportion of screen time for films of a specified origin other than that of the contracting party imposing such screen quotas; *Provided* that no such minimum proportion of screen time shall be increased above the level in effect on April 10, 1947;

(d) Screen quotas shall be subject to negotiation for their limitation, liberalization or elimination.

Article V

Freedom of Transit

1. Goods (including baggage), and also vessels and other means of transport, shall be deemed to be in transit across the territory of a contracting party when the passage across such territory, with or without trans-shipment, warehousing, breaking bulk, or change in the mode of transport, is only a portion of a complete journey beginning and terminating beyond the frontier of the contracting party across whose territory the traffic passes. Traffic of this nature is termed in this Article " traffic in transit ".

2. There shall be freedom of transit through the territory of each contracting party, via the routes most convenient for international transit, for traffic in transit to or from the territory of other contracting parties. No distinction shall be made which is based on the flag of vessels, the place of origin, departure, entry, exit or destination, or on any circumstances relating to the ownership of goods, of vessels or of other means of transport.

3. Any contracting party may require that traffic in transit through its territory be entered at the proper custom house, but, except in cases of failure to comply with applicable customs laws and regulations, such traffic coming from or going to the territory of other contracting parties shall not be subject to any unnecessary delays or restrictions and shall be exempt from customs duties and from all transit duties or other charges imposed in respect of transit, except charges for transportation or those commensurate with administrative expenses entailed by transit or with the cost of services rendered.

4. All charges and regulations imposed by contracting parties on traffic in transit to or from the territories of other contracting parties shall be reasonable, having regard to the conditions of the traffic.

5. With respect to all charges, regulations and formalities in connection with transit, each contracting party shall accord to traffic in transit to or from the territory of any other contracting party treatment no less favourable than the treatment accorded to traffic in transit to or from any third country.*

6. Each contracting party shall accord to products which have been in transit through the territory of any other contracting party treatment no less favourable than that which would have been accorded to such products had they been transported from their place of origin to their destination without going through the territory of such other contracting party. Any contracting party shall, however, be free to maintain its requirements of direct consignment existing on the date of this Agreement, in respect of any goods in regard to which such direct consignment is a requisite condition of eligibility for entry of the goods at preferential rates of duty or has relation to the contracting party's prescribed method of valuation for duty purposes.

7. The provisions of this Article shall not apply to the operation of aircraft in transit, but shall apply to air transit of goods (including baggage).

Article VI

Anti-dumping and Countervailing Duties

1. The contracting parties recognize that dumping, by which products of one country are introduced into the commerce of another country at less than the normal value of the products, is to be condemned if it causes or threatens material injury to an established industry in the territory of a contracting party or materially retards the establishment of a domestic industry. For the purposes of this Article, a product is to be considered as being introduced into the commerce of an importing country at less than its normal value, if the price of the product exported from one country to another

   (a) is less than the comparable price, in the ordinary course of trade, for the like product when destined for consumption in the exporting country, or,

   (b) in the absence of such domestic price, is less than either

       (i) the highest comparable price for the like product for export to any third country in the ordinary course of trade, or

       (ii) the cost of production of the product in the country of origin plus a reasonable addition for selling cost and profit.

Due allowance shall be made in each case for differences in conditions and terms of sale, for differences in taxation, and for other differences affecting price comparability.*

2. In order to offset or prevent dumping, a contracting party may levy on any dumped product an anti-dumping duty not greater in amount than the margin of dumping in respect of such product. For the purposes of this Article, the margin of dumping is the price difference determined in accordance with the provisions of paragraph 1.*

3. No countervailing duty shall be levied on any product of the territory of any contracting party imported into the territory of another contracting party in excess of an amount equal to the estimated bounty or subsidy determined to have been granted, directly or indirectly, on the manufacture, production or export of such product in the country of origin or exportation, including any special subsidy to the transportation of a particular product. The term " countervailing duty " shall be understood to mean a special duty levied for the purpose of offsetting any bounty or subsidy bestowed, directly or indirectly, upon the manufacture, production or export of any merchandise.*

4.   No product of the territory of any contracting party imported into the territory of any other contracting party shall be subject to anti-dumping or countervailing duty by reason of the exemption of such product from duties or taxes borne by the like product when destined for consumption in the country of origin or exportation, or by reason of the refund of such duties or taxes.

5.   No product of the territory of any contracting party imported into the territory of any other contracting party shall be subject to both anti-dumping and countervailing duties to compensate for the same situation of dumping or export subsidization.

6.   (a)   No contracting party shall levy any anti-dumping or counter-vailing duty on the importation of any product of the territory of another contracting party unless it determines that the effect of the dumping or subsidization, as the case may be, is such as to cause or threaten material injury to an established domestic industry, or is such as to retard materially the establishment of a domestic industry.

(b)   The CONTRACTING PARTIES may waive the requirement of sub-paragraph (a) of this paragraph so as to permit a contracting party to levy an anti-dumping or countervailing duty on the importation of any product for the purpose of offsetting dumping or subsidization which causes or threatens material injury to an industry in the territory of another contract-ing party exporting the product concerned to the territory of the importing contracting party.   The CONTRACTING PARTIES shall waive the requirements of sub-paragraph (a) of this paragraph, so as to permit the levying of a countervailing duty, in cases in which they find that a subsidy is causing or threatening material injury to an industry in the territory of another contracting party exporting the product concerned to the territory of the importing contracting party.*

(c)   In exceptional circumstances, however, where delay might cause damage which would be difficult to repair, a contracting party may levy a countervailing duty for the purpose referred to in sub-paragraph (b) of this paragraph without the prior approval of the CONTRACTING PARTIES; *Provided* that such action shall be reported immediately to the CONTRACTING PARTIES and that the countervailing duty shall be withdrawn promptly if the CONTRACTING PARTIES disapprove.

7.   A system for the stabilization of the domestic price or of the return to domestic producers of a primary commodity, independently of the move-ments of export prices, which results at times in the sale of the commodity for export at a price lower than the comparable price charged for the like commodity to buyers in the domestic market, shall be presumed not to result in material injury within the meaning of paragraph 6 if it is determined

by consultation among the contracting parties substantially interested in the commodity concerned that:

(*a*) the system has also resulted in the sale of the commodity for export at a price higher than the comparable price charged for the like commodity to buyers in the domestic market, and

(*b*) the system is so operated, either because of the effective regulation of production, or otherwise, as not to stimulate exports unduly or otherwise seriously prejudice the interests of other contracting parties.

Article VII

Valuation for Customs Purposes

1. The contracting parties recognize the validity of the general principles of valuation set forth in the following paragraphs of this Article, and they undertake to give effect to such principles, in respect of all products subject to duties or other charges * or restrictions on importation and exportation based upon or regulated in any manner by value. Moreover, they shall, upon a request by another contracting party review the operation of any of their laws or regulations relating to value for customs purposes in the light of these principles. The CONTRACTING PARTIES may request from contracting parties reports on steps taken by them in pursuance of the provisions of this Article.

2. (*a*) The value for customs purposes of imported merchandise should be based on the actual value of the imported merchandise on which duty is assessed, or of like merchandise, and should not be based on the value of merchandise of national origin or on arbitrary or fictitious values.*

(*b*) "Actual value" should be the price at which, at a time and place determined by the legislation of the country of importation, such or like merchandise is sold or offered for sale in the ordinary course of trade under fully competitive conditions. To the extent to which the price of such or like merchandise is governed by the quantity in a particular transaction, the price to be considered should uniformly be related to either (i) comparable quantities, or (ii) quantities not less favourable to importers than those in which the greater volume of the merchandise is sold in the trade between the countries of exportation and importation.*

(*c*) When the actual value is not ascertainable in accordance with sub-paragraph (*b*) of this paragraph, the value for customs purposes should be based on the nearest ascertainable equivalent of such value.*

3. The value for customs purposes of any imported product should not include the amount of any internal tax, applicable within the country of

origin or export, from which the imported product has been exempted or has been or will be relieved by means of refund.

4. (*a*) Except as otherwise provided for in this paragraph, where it is necessary for the purposes of paragraph 2 of this Article for a contracting party to convert into its own currency a price expressed in the currency of another country, the conversion rate of exchange to be used shall be based, for each currency involved, on the par value as established pursuant to the Articles of Agreement of the International Monetary Fund or on the rate of exchange recognized by the Fund, or on the par value established in accordance with a special exchange agreement entered into pursuant to Article XV of this Agreement.

(*b*) Where no such established par value and no such recognized rate of exchange exist, the conversion rate shall reflect effectively the current value of such currency in commercial transactions.

(*c*) The CONTRACTING PARTIES, in agreement with the International Monetary Fund, shall formulate rules governing the conversion by contracting parties of any foreign currency in respect of which multiple rates of exchange are maintained consistently with the Articles of Agreement of the International Monetary Fund. Any contracting party may apply such rules in respect of such foreign currencies for the purposes of paragraph 2 of this Article as an alternative to the use of par values. Until such rules are adopted by the CONTRACTING PARTIES, any contracting party may employ, in respect of any such foreign currency, rules of conversion for the purposes of paragraph 2 of this Article which are designed to reflect effectively the value of such foreign currency in commercial transactions.

(*d*) Nothing in this paragraph shall be construed to require any contracting party to alter the method of converting currencies for customs purposes which is applicable in its territory on the date of this Agreement, if such alteration would have the effect of increasing generally the amounts of duty payable.

5. The bases and methods for determining the value of products subject to duties or other charges or restrictions based upon or regulated in any manner by value should be stable and should be given sufficient publicity to enable traders to estimate, with a reasonable degree of certainty, the value for customs purposes.

Article VIII

Fees and Formalities connected with Importation and Exportation *

1. (*a*) All fees and charges of whatever character (other than import and export duties and other than taxes within the purview of Article III) imposed by contracting parties on or in connexion with importation or exportation shall be limited in amount to the approximate cost of services rendered and shall not represent an indirect protection to domestic products or a taxation of imports or exports for fiscal purposes.

(*b*) The contracting parties recognize the need for reducing the number and diversity of fees and charges referred to in sub-paragraph (*a*).

(*c*) The contracting parties also recognize the need for minimizing the incidence and complexity of import and export formalities and for decreasing and simplifying import and export documentation requirements.*

2. A contracting party shall, upon request by another contracting party or by the CONTRACTING PARTIES, review the operation of its laws and regulations in the light of the provisions of this Article.

3. No contracting party shall impose substantial penalties for minor breaches of customs regulations or procedural requirements.   In particular, no penalty in respect of any omission or mistake in customs documentation which is easily rectifiable and obviously made without fraudulent intent or gross negligence shall be greater than necessary to serve merely as a warning.

4. The provisions of this Article shall extend to fees, charges, formalities and requirements imposed by governmental authorities in connexion with importation and exportation, including those relating to:

(*a*) consular transactions, such as consular invoices and certificates;

(*b*) quantitative restrictions;

(*c*) licensing;

(*d*) exchange control;

(*e*) statistical services;

(*f*) documents, documentation and certification;

(*g*) analysis and inspection; and

(*h*) quarantine, sanitation and fumigation.

Article IX

Marks of Origin

1. Each contracting party shall accord to the products of the territories of other contracting parties treatment with regard to marking requirements no less favourable than the treatment accorded to like products of any third country.

2. The contracting parties recognize that, in adopting and enforcing laws and regulations relating to marks of origin, the difficulties and inconveniences which such measures may cause to the commerce and industry of exporting countries should be reduced to a minimum, due regard being had to the necessity of protecting consumers against fraudulent or misleading indications.

3. Whenever it is administratively practicable to do so, contracting parties should permit required marks of origin to be affixed at the time of importation.

4. The laws and regulations of contracting parties relating to the marking of imported products shall be such as to permit compliance without seriously damaging the products, or materially reducing their value, or unreasonably increasing their cost.

5. As a general rule, no special duty or penalty should be imposed by any contracting party for failure to comply with marking requirements prior to importation unless corrective marking is unreasonably delayed or deceptive marks have been affixed or the required marking has been intentionally omitted.

6. The contracting parties shall co-operate with each other with a view to preventing the use of trade names in such manner as to misrepresent the true origin of a product, to the detriment of such distinctive regional or geographical names of products of the territory of a contracting party as are protected by its. legislation. Each contracting party shall accord full and sympathetic consideration to such requests or representations as may be made by any other contracting party regarding the application of the undertaking set forth in the preceding sentence to names of products which have been communicated to it by the other contracting party.

Article X

Publication and Administration of Trade Regulations

1. Laws, regulations, judicial decisions and administrative rulings of general application, made effective by any contracting party, pertaining to the classification or the valuation of products for customs purposes, or to rates of duty, taxes or other charges, or to requirements, restrictions or prohibitions on imports or exports or on the transfer of payments therefor, or affecting their sale, distribution, transportation, insurance, warehousing, inspection, exhibition, processing, mixing or other use, shall be published promptly in such a manner as to enable governments and traders to become acquainted with them. Agreements affecting international trade policy which are in force between the government or a governmental agency of any contracting party and the government or governmental agency of any other contracting party shall also be published. The provisions of this paragraph shall not require any contracting party to disclose confidential information which would impede law enforcement or otherwise be contrary to the public interest or would prejudice the legitimate commercial interests of particular enterprises, public or private.

2. No measure of general application taken by any contracting party effecting an advance in a rate of duty or other charge on imports under an established and uniform practice, or imposing a new or more burdensome requirement, restriction or prohibition on imports, or on the transfer of payments therefor, shall be enforced before such measure has been officially published.

3. (*a*) Each contracting party shall administer in a uniform, impartial and reasonable manner all its laws, regulations, decisions and rulings of the kind described in paragraph 1 of this Article.

(*b*) Each contracting party shall maintain, or institute as soon as practicable, judicial, arbitral or administrative tribunals or procedures for the purpose, *inter alia*, of the prompt review and correction of administrative action relating to customs matters. Such tribunals or procedures shall be independent of the agencies entrusted with administrative enforcement and their decisions shall be implemented by, and shall govern the practice of, such agencies unless an appeal is lodged with a court or tribunal of superior jurisdiction within the time prescribed for appeals to be lodged by importers; *Provided* that the central administration of such agency may take steps to obtain a review of the matter in another proceeding if there is good cause to believe that the decision is inconsistent with established principles of law or the actual facts.

114

(*c*) The provisions of sub-paragraph (*b*) of this paragraph shall not require the elimination or substitution of procedures in force in the territory of a contracting party on the date of this Agreement which in fact provide for an objective and impartial review of administrative action even though such procedures are not fully or formally independent of the agencies entrusted with administrative enforcement. Any contracting party employing such procedures shall, upon request, furnish the CONTRACTING PARTIES with full information thereon in order that they may determine whether such procedures conform to the requirements of this sub-paragraph.

Article XI *

General Elimination of Quantitative Restrictions

1. No prohibitions or restrictions other than duties, taxes or other charges, whether made effective through quotas, import or export licences or other measures, shall be instituted or maintained by any contracting party on the importation of any product of the territory of any other contracting party or on the exportation or sale for export of any product destined for the territory of any other contracting party.

2. The provisions of paragraph 1 of this Article shall not extend to the following:

(*a*) Export prohibitions or restrictions temporarily applied to prevent or relieve critical shortages of foodstuffs or other products essential to the exporting contracting party;

(*b*) Import and export prohibitions or restrictions necessary to the application of standards or regulations for the classification, grading or marketing of commodities in international trade;

(*c*) Import restrictions on any agricultural or fisheries product, imported in any form,* necessary to the enforcement of governmental measures which operate:

(i) to restrict the quantities of the like domestic product permitted to be marketed or produced, or, if there is no substantial domestic production of the like product, of a domestic product for which the imported product can be directly substituted; or

(ii) to remove a temporary surplus of the like domestic product, or, if there is no substantial domestic production of the like product, of a domestic product for which the imported product can be directly substituted, by making the surplus available to certain groups of domestic consumers free of charge or at prices below the current market level; or

(iii) to restrict the quantities permitted to be produced of any animal product the production of which is directly dependent, wholly or mainly, on the imported commodity, if the domestic production of that commodity is relatively negligible.

Any contracting party applying restrictions on the importation of any product pursuant to sub-paragraph (c) of this paragraph shall give public notice of the total quantity or value of the product permitted to be imported during a specified future period and of any change in such quantity or value. Moreover, any restrictions applied under (i) above shall not be such as will reduce the total of imports relative to the total of domestic production, as compared with the proportion which might reasonably be expected to rule between the two in the absence of restrictions. In determining this proportion, the contracting party shall pay due regard to the proportion prevailing during a previous representative period and to any special factors* which may have affected or may be affecting the trade in the product concerned.

Article XII *

Restrictions to Safeguard the Balance of Payments

1. Notwithstanding the provisions of paragraph 1 of Article XI, any contracting party, in order to safeguard its external financial position and its balance of payments, may restrict the quantity or value of merchandise permitted to be imported, subject to the provisions of the following paragraphs of this Article.

2. (a) Import restrictions instituted, maintained or intensified by a contracting party under this Article shall not exceed those necessary:

(i) to forestall the imminent threat of, or to stop, a serious decline in its monetary reserves, or

(ii) in the case of a contracting party with very low monetary reserves, to achieve a reasonable rate of increase in its reserves.

Due regard shall be paid in either case to any special factors which may be affecting the reserves of such contracting party or its need for reserves, including, where special external credits or other resources are available to it, the need to provide for the appropriate use of such credits or resources.

(b) Contracting parties applying restrictions under sub-paragraph (a) of this paragraph shall progressively relax them as such conditions improve, maintaining them only to the extent that the conditions specified in that sub-paragraph still justify their application. They shall eliminate the restrictions when conditions would no longer justify their institution or maintenance under that sub-paragraph.

3. (*a*) Contracting parties undertake, in carrying out their domestic policies, to pay due regard to the need for maintaining or restoring equilibrium in their balance of payments on a sound and lasting basis and to the desirability of avoiding an uneconomic employment of productive resources. They recognize that, in order to achieve these ends, it is desirable so far as possible to adopt measures which expand rather than contract international trade.

(*b*) Contracting parties applying restrictions under this Article may determine the incidence of the restrictions on imports of different products or classes of products in such a way as to give priority to the importation of those products which are more essential.

(*c*) Contracting parties applying restrictions under this Article undertake:

> (i) to avoid unnecessary damage to the commercial or economic interests of any other contracting party;*
>
> (ii) not to apply restrictions so as to prevent unreasonably the importation of any description of goods in minimum commercial quantities the exclusion of which would impair regular channels of trade; and
>
> (iii) not to apply restrictions which would prevent the importation of commercial samples or prevent compliance with patent, trade mark, copyright, or similar procedures.

(*d*) The contracting parties recognize that, as a result of domestic policies directed towards the achievement and maintenance of full and productive employment or towards the development of economic resources, a contracting party may experience a high level of demand for imports involving a threat to its monetary reserves of the sort referred to in paragraph 2 (*a*) of this Article. Accordingly, a contracting party otherwise complying with the provisions of this Article shall not be required to withdraw or modify restrictions on the ground that a change in those policies would render unnecessary restrictions which it is applying under this Article.

4. (*a*) Any contracting party applying new restrictions or raising the general level of its existing restrictions by a substantial intensification of the measures applied under this Article shall immediately after instituting or intensifying such restrictions (or, in circumstances in which prior consultation is practicable, before doing so) consult with the CONTRACTING

PARTIES as to the nature of its balance of payments difficulties, alternative corrective measures which may be available, and the possible effect of the restrictions on the economies of other contracting parties.

(*b*) On a date to be determined by them,* the CONTRACTING PARTIES shall review all restrictions still applied under this Article on that date. Beginning one year after that date, contracting parties applying import restrictions under this Article shall enter into consultations of the type provided for in sub-paragraph (*a*) of this paragraph with the CONTRACTING PARTIES annually.

(*c*) (i) If, in the course of consultations with a contracting party under sub-paragraph (*a*) or (*b*) above, the CONTRACTING PARTIES find that the restrictions are not consistent with the provisions of this Article or with those of Article XIII (subject to the provisions of Article XIV), they shall indicate the nature of the inconsistency and may advise that the restrictions be suitably modified.

(ii) If, however, as a result of the consultations, the CONTRACTING PARTIES determine that the restrictions are being applied in a manner involving an inconsistency of a serious nature with the provisions of this Article or with those of Article XIII (subject to the provisions of Article XIV) and that damage to the trade of any contracting party is caused or threatened thereby, they shall so inform the contracting party applying the restrictions and shall make appropriate recommendations for securing conformity with such provisions within a specified period of time. If such contracting party does not comply with these recommendations within the specified period, the CONTRACTING PARTIES may release any contracting party the trade of which is adversely affected by the restrictions from such obligations under this Agreement towards the contracting party applying the restrictions as they determine to be appropriate in the circumstances.

(*d*) The CONTRACTING PARTIES shall invite any contracting party which is applying restrictions under this Article to enter into consultations with them at the request of any contracting party which can establish a *prima facie* case that the restrictions are inconsistent with the provisions of this Article or with those of Article XIII (subject to the provisions of Article XIV) and that its trade is adversely affected thereby. However, no such invitation shall be issued unless the CONTRACTING PARTIES have ascertained that direct discussions between the contracting parties concerned have not been successful. If, as a result of the consultations with the CONTRACTING PARTIES, no agreement is reached and they determine that the restrictions are being applied inconsistently with such provisions, and that damage to the trade of the contracting party initiating the procedure is caused or threatened thereby, they shall recommend the withdrawal or modification of the restrictions. If the restrictions are not withdrawn or modified

118

within such time as the CONTRACTING PARTIES may prescribe, they may release the contracting party initiating the procedure from such obligations under this Agreement towards the contracting party applying the restrictions as they determine to be appropriate in the circumstances.

(e) In proceeding under this paragraph, the CONTRACTING PARTIES shall have due regard to any special external factors adversely affecting the export trade of the contracting party applying restrictions.*

(f) Determinations under this paragraph shall be rendered expeditiously and, if possible, within sixty days of the initiation of the consultations.

5. If there is a persistent and widespread application of import restrictions under this Article, indicating the existence of a general disequilibrium which is restricting international trade, the CONTRACTING PARTIES shall initiate discussions to consider whether other measures might be taken, either by those contracting parties the balances of payments of which are under pressure or by those the balances of payments of which are tending to be exceptionally favourable, or by any appropriate intergovernmental organization, to remove the underlying causes of the disequilibrium. On the invitation of the CONTRACTING PARTIES, contracting parties shall participate in such discussions.

Article XIII *

Non-discriminatory Administration of Quantitative Restrictions

1. No prohibition or restriction shall be applied by any contracting party on the importation of any product of the territory of any other contracting party or on the exportation of any product destined for the territory of any other contracting party, unless the importation of the like product of all third countries or the exportation of the like product to all third countries is similarly prohibited or restricted.

2. In applying import restrictions to any product, contracting parties shall aim at a distribution of trade in such product approaching as closely as possible the shares which the various contracting parties might be expected to obtain in the absence of such restrictions, and to this end shall observe the following provisions:

(a) Wherever practicable, quotas representing the total amount of permitted imports (whether allocated among supplying countries or not) shall be fixed, and notice given of their amount in accordance with paragraph 3 (b) of this Article;

(b) In cases in which quotas are not practicable, the restrictions may be applied by means of import licences or permits without a quota;

119

(c) Contracting parties shall not, except for purposes of operating quotas allocated in accordance with sub-paragraph (d) of this paragraph, require that import licences or permits be utilized for the importation of the product concerned from a particular country or source;

(d) In cases in which a quota is allocated among supplying countries, the contracting party applying the restrictions may seek agreement with respect to the allocation of shares in the quota with all other contracting parties having a substantial interest in supplying the product concerned. In cases in which this method is not reasonably practicable, the contracting party concerned shall allot to contracting parties having a substantial interest in supplying the product shares based upon the proportions, supplied by such contracting parties during a previous representative period, of the total quantity or value of imports of the product, due account being taken of any special factors which may have affected or may be affecting the trade in the product. No conditions or formalities shall be imposed which would prevent any contracting party from utilizing fully the share of any such total quantity or value which has been allotted to it, subject to importation being made within any prescribed period to which the quota may relate.*

3. (a) In cases in which import licences are issued in connection with import restrictions, the contracting party applying the restrictions shall provide, upon the request of any contracting party having an interest in the trade in the product concerned, all relevant information concerning the administration of the restrictions, the import licences granted over a recent period and the distribution of such licences among supplying countries; *Provided* that there shall be no obligation to supply information as to the names of importing or supplying enterprises.

(b) In the case of import restrictions involving the fixing of quotas, the contracting party applying the restrictions shall give public notice of the total quantity or value of the product or products which will be permitted to be imported during a specified future period and of any change in such quantity or value. Any supplies of the product in question which were *en route* at the time at which public notice was given shall not be excluded from entry; *Provided* that they may be counted so far as practicable, against the quantity permitted to be imported in the period in question, and also, where necessary, against the quantities permitted to be imported in the next following period or periods; and *Provided* further that if any contracting party customarily exempts from such restrictions products entered for consumption or withdrawn from warehouse for consumption during a period of thirty days after the day of such public notice, such practice shall be considered full compliance with this sub-paragraph.

(*c*) In the case of quotas allocated among supplying countries, the contracting party applying the restrictions shall promptly inform all other contracting parties having an interest in supplying the product concerned of the shares in the quota currently allocated, by quantity or value, to the various supplying countries and shall give public notice thereof.

4. With regard to restrictions applied in accordance with paragraph 2 (*d*) of this Article or under paragraph 2 (*c*) of Article XI, the selection of a representative period for any product and the appraisal of any special factors * affecting the trade in the product shall be made initially by the contracting party applying the restriction; *Provided* that such contracting party shall, upon the request of any other contracting party having a substantial interest in supplying that product or upon the request of the CONTRACTING PARTIES, consult promptly with the other contracting party or the CONTRACTING PARTIES regarding the need for an adjustment of the proportion determined or of the base period selected, or for the reappraisal of the special factors involved, or for the elimination of conditions, formalities or any other provisions established unilaterally relating to the allocation of an adequate quota or its unrestricted utilization.

5. The provisions of this Article shall apply to any tariff quota instituted or maintained by any contracting party, and, in so far as applicable, the principles of this Article shall also extend to export restrictions.

Article XIV *

Exceptions to the Rule of Non-discrimination

1. A contracting party which applies restrictions under Article XII or under Section B of Article XVIII may, in the application of such restrictions, deviate from the provisions of Article XIII in a manner having equivalent effect to restrictions on payments and transfers for current international transactions which that contracting party may at that time apply under Article VIII or XIV of the Articles of Agreement of the International Monetary Fund, or under analogous provisions of a special exchange agreement entered into pursuant to paragraph 6 of Article XV.*

2. A contracting party which is applying import restrictions under Article XII or under Section B of Article XVIII may, with the consent of the CONTRACTING PARTIES, temporarily deviate from the provisions of Article XIII in respect of a small part of its external trade where the benefits to the contracting party or contracting parties concerned substantially outweigh any injury which may result to the trade of other contracting parties.*

3.   The provisions of Article XIII shall not preclude a group of territories having a common quota in the International Monetary Fund from applying against imports from other countries, but not among themselves, restrictions in accordance with the provisions of Article XII or of Section B of Article XVIII on condition that such restrictions are in all other respects consistent with the provisions of Article XIII.

4.   A contracting party applying import restrictions under Article XII or under Section B of Article XVIII shall not be precluded by Articles XI to XV or Section B of Article XVIII of this Agreement from applying measures to direct its exports in such a manner as to increase its earnings of currencies which it can use without deviation from the provisions of Article XIII.

5.   A contracting party shall not be precluded by Articles XI to XV, inclusive, or by Section B of Article XVIII, of this Agreement from applying quantitative restrictions:

  (a)   having equivalent effect to exchange restrictions authorized under Section 3 (b) of Article VII of the Articles of Agreement of the International Monetary Fund, or

  (b)   under the preferential arrangements provided for in Annex A of this Agreement, pending the outcome of the negotiations referred to therein.

Article XV

Exchange Arrangements

1.   The CONTRACTING PARTIES shall seek co-operation with the International Monetary Fund to the end that the CONTRACTING PARTIES and the Fund may pursue a co-ordinated policy with regard to exchange questions within the jurisdiction of the Fund and questions of quantitative restrictions and other trade measures within the jurisdiction of the CONTRACTING PARTIES.

2.   In all cases in which the CONTRACTING PARTIES are called upon to consider or deal with problems concerning monetary reserves, balances of payments or foreign exchange arrangements, they shall consult fully with the International Monetary Fund. In such consultations, the CONTRACTING PARTIES shall accept all findings of statistical and other facts presented by the Fund relating to foreign exchange, monetary reserves and balances of payments, and shall accept the determination of the Fund as to whether action by a contracting party in exchange matters is in accordance with the Articles of Agreement of the International Monetary Fund,

122

or with the terms of a special exchange agreement between that contracting party and the CONTRACTING PARTIES. The CONTRACTING PARTIES, in reaching their final decision in cases involving the criteria set forth in paragraph 2 (*a*) of Article XII or in paragraph 9 of Article XVIII, shall accept the determination of the Fund as to what constitutes a serious decline in the contracting party's monetary reserves, a very low level of its monetary reserves or a reasonable rate of increase in its monetary reserves, and as to the financial aspects of other matters covered in consultation in such cases.

3. The CONTRACTING PARTIES shall seek agreement with the Fund regarding procedures for consultation under paragraph 2 of this Article.

4. Contracting parties shall not, by exchange action, frustrate * the intent of the provisions of this Agreement, nor, by trade action, the intent of the provisions of the Articles of Agreement of the International Monetary Fund.

5. If the CONTRACTING PARTIES consider, at any time, that exchange restrictions on payments and transfers in connexion with imports are being applied by a contracting party in a manner inconsistent with the exceptions provided for in this Agreement for quantitative restrictions, they shall report thereon to the Fund.

6. Any contracting party which is not a member of the Fund shall, within a time to be determined by the CONTRACTING PARTIES after consultation with the Fund, become a member of the Fund, or, failing that, enter into a special exchange agreement with the CONTRACTING PARTIES. A contracting party which ceases to be a member of the Fund shall forthwith enter into a special exchange agreement with the CONTRACTING PARTIES. Any special exchange agreement entered into by a contracting party under this paragraph shall thereupon become part of its obligations under this Agreement.

7. (*a*) A special exchange agreement between a contracting party and the CONTRACTING PARTIES under paragraph 6 of this Article shall provide to the satisfaction of the CONTRACTING PARTIES that the objectives of this Agreement will not be frustrated as a result of action in exchange matters by the contracting party in question.

(*b*) The terms of any such agreement shall not impose obligations on the contracting party in exchange matters generally more restrictive than those imposed by the Articles of Agreement of the International Monetary Fund on members of the Fund.

8. A contracting party which is not a member of the Fund shall furnish such information within the general scope of section 5 of Article VIII of the Articles of Agreement of the International Monetary Fund as

the CONTRACTING PARTIES may require in order to carry out their functions under this Agreement.

9. Nothing in this Agreement shall preclude:

(a) the use by a contracting party of exchange controls or exchange restrictions in accordance with the Articles of Agreement of the International Monetary Fund or with that contracting party's special exchange agreement with the CONTRACTING PARTIES, or

(b) the use by a contracting party of restrictions or controls on imports or exports, the sole effect of which, additional to the effects permitted under Articles XI, XII, XIII and XIV, is to make effective such exchange controls or exchange restrictions.

Article XVI *

Subsidies

Section A—Subsidies in General

1. If any contracting party grants or maintains any subsidy, including any form of income or price support, which operates directly or indirectly to increase exports of any product from, or to reduce imports of any product into, its territory, it shall notify the CONTRACTING PARTIES in writing of the extent and nature of the subsidization, of the estimated effect of the subsidization on the quantity of the affected product or products imported into or exported from its territory and of the circumstances making the subsidization necessary. In any case in which it is determined that serious prejudice to the interests of any other contracting party is caused or threatened by any such subsidization, the contracting party granting the subsidy shall, upon request, discuss with the other contracting party or parties concerned, or with the CONTRACTING PARTIES, the possibility of limiting the subsidization.

Section B—Additional Provisions on Export Subsidies *

2. The contracting parties recognize that the granting by a contracting party of a subsidy on the export of any product may have harmful effects for other contracting parties, both importing and exporting, may cause undue disturbance to their normal commercial interests, and may hinder the achievement of the objectives of this Agreement.

3. Accordingly, contracting parties should seek to avoid the use of subsidies on the export of primary products. If, however, a contracting

party grants directly or indirectly any form of subsidy which operates to increase the export of any primary product from its territory, such subsidy shall not be applied in a manner which results in that contracting party having more than an equitable share of world export trade in that product, account being taken of the shares of the contracting parties in such trade in the product during a previous representative period, and any special factors which may have affected or may be affecting such trade in the product.*

4. Further, as from 1 January 1958 or the earliest practicable date thereafter, contracting parties shall cease to grant either directly or indirectly any form of subsidy on the export of any product other than a primary product which subsidy results in the sale of such product for export at a price lower than the comparable price charged for the like product to buyers in the domestic market. Until 31 December 1957 no contracting party shall extend the scope of any such subsidization beyond that existing on 1 January 1955 by the introduction of new, or the extension of existing, subsidies.*

5. The CONTRACTING PARTIES shall review the operation of the provisions of this Article from time to time with a view to examining its effectiveness, in the light of actual experience, in promoting the objectives of this Agreement and avoiding subsidization seriously prejudicial to the trade or interests of contracting parties.

Article XVII

State Trading Enterprises

1.* (a) Each contracting party undertakes that if it establishes or maintains a State enterprise, wherever located, or grants to any enterprise, formally or in effect, exclusive or special privileges,* such enterprise shall, in its purchases or sales involving either imports or exports, act in a manner consistent with the general principles of non-discriminatory treatment prescribed in this Agreement for governmental measures affecting imports or exports by private traders.

(b) The provisions of sub-paragraph (a) of this paragraph shall be understood to require that such enterprises shall, having due regard to the other provisions of this Agreement, make any such purchases or sales solely in accordance with commercial considerations,* including price, quality, availability, marketability, transportation and other conditions of purchase or sale, and shall afford the enterprises of the other contracting parties adequate opportunity, in accordance with customary business practice, to compete for participation in such purchases or sales.

(*c*) No contracting party shall prevent any enterprise (whether or not an enterprise described in sub-paragraph (*a*) of this paragraph) under its jurisdiction from acting in accordance with the principles of sub-paragraphs (*a*) and (*b*) of this paragraph.

2. The provisions of paragraph 1 of this Article shall not apply to imports of products for immediate or ultimate consumption in governmental use and not otherwise for resale or use in the production of goods * for sale. With respect to such imports, each contracting party shall accord to the trade of the other contracting parties fair and equitable treatment.

3. The contracting parties recognize that enterprises of the kind described in paragraph 1 (*a*) of this Article might be operated so as to create serious obstacles to trade; thus negotiations on a reciprocal and mutually advantageous basis designed to limit or reduce such obstacles are of importance to the expansion of international trade.*

4. (*a*) Contracting parties shall notify the CONTRACTING PARTIES of the products which are imported into or exported from their territories by enterprises of the kind described in paragraph 1 (*a*) of this Article.

(*b*) A contracting party establishing, maintaining or authorizing an import monopoly of a product, which is not the subject of a concession under Article II, shall, on the request of another contracting party having a substantial trade in the product concerned, inform the CONTRACTING PARTIES of the import mark-up * on the product during a recent representative period, or, when it is not possible to do so, of the price charged on the resale of the product.

(*c*) The CONTRACTING PARTIES may, at the request of a contracting party which has reason to believe that its interests under this Agreement are being adversely affected by the operations of an enterprise of the kind described in paragraph 1 (*a*), request the contracting party establishing, maintaining or authorizing such enterprise to supply information about its operations related to the carrying out of the provisions of this Agreement.

(*d*) The provisions of this paragraph shall not require any contracting party to disclose confidential information which would impede law enforcement or otherwise be contrary to the public interest or would prejudice the legitimate commercial interests of particular enterprises.

Article XVIII *

Governmental Assistance to Economic Development

1. The contracting parties recognize that the attainment of the objectives of this Agreement will be facilitated by the progressive development

of their economies, particularly of those contracting parties the economies of which can only support low standards of living* and are in the early stages of development.*

2. The contracting parties recognize further that it may be necessary for those contracting parties, in order to implement programmes and policies of economic development designed to raise the general standard of living of their people, to take protective or other measures affecting imports, and that such measures are justified in so far as they facilitate the attainment of the objectives of this Agreement. They agree, therefore, that those contracting parties should enjoy additional facilities to enable them (a) to maintain sufficient flexibility in their tariff structure to be able to grant the tariff protection required for the establishment of a particular industry * and (b) to apply quantitative restrictions for balance of payments purposes in a manner which takes full account of the continued high level of demand for imports likely to be generated by their programmes of economic development.

3. The contracting parties recognize finally that, with those additional facilities which are provided for in Sections A and B of this Article, the provisions of this Agreement would normally be sufficient to enable contracting parties to meet the requirements of their economic development. They agree, however, that there may be circumstances where no measure consistent with those provisions is practicable to permit a contracting party in the process of economic development to grant the governmental assistance required to promote the establishment of particular industries * with a view to raising the general standard of living of its people. Special procedures are laid down in Sections C and D of this Article to deal with those cases.

4. (a) Consequently, a contracting party the economy of which can only support low standards of living * and is in the early stages of development * shall be free to deviate temporarily from the provisions of the other Articles of this Agreement, as provided in Sections A, B and C of this Article.

(b) A contracting party the economy of which is in the process of development, but which does not come within the scope of sub-paragraph (a) above, may submit applications to the CONTRACTING PARTIES under Section D of this Article.

5. The contracting parties recognize that the export earnings of contracting parties, the economies of which are of the type described in paragraph 4 (a) and (b) above and which depend on exports of a small number of primary commodities, may be seriously reduced by a decline in the sale of such commodities. Accordingly, when the exports of primary commodities by such a contracting party are seriously affected by measures taken

by another contracting party, it may have resort to the consultation provisions of Article XXII of this Agreement.

6. The Contracting Parties shall review annually all measures applied pursuant to the provisions of Sections C and D of this Article.

Section A

7. (a) If a contracting party coming within the scope of paragraph 4 (a) of this Article considers it desirable, in order to promote the establishment of a particular industry * with a view to raising the general standard of living of its people, to modify or withdraw a concession included in the appropriate Schedule annexed to this Agreement, it shall notify the Contracting Parties to this effect and enter into negotiations with any contracting party with which such concession was initially negotiated, and with any other contracting party determined by the Contracting Parties to have a substantial interest therein. If agreement is reached between such contracting parties concerned, they shall be free to modify or withdraw concessions under the appropriate Schedules to this Agreement in order to give effect to such agreement, including any compensatory adjustments involved.

(b) If agreement is not reached within sixty days after the notification provided for in sub-paragraph (a) above, the contracting party which proposes to modify or withdraw the concession may refer the matter to the Contracting Parties, which shall promptly examine it. If they find that the contracting party which proposes to modify or withdraw the concession has made every effort to reach an agreement and that the compensatory adjustment offered by it is adequate, that contracting party shall be free to modify or withdraw the concession if, at the same time, it gives effect to the compensatory adjustment. If the Contracting Parties do not find that the compensation offered by a contracting party proposing to modify or withdraw the concession is adequate, but find that it has made every reasonable effort to offer adequate compensation, that contracting party shall be free to proceed with such modification or withdrawal. If such action is taken, any other contracting party referred to in sub-paragraph (a) above shall be free to modify or withdraw substantially equivalent concessions initially negotiated with the contracting party which has taken the action.*

Section B

8. The contracting parties recognize that contracting parties coming within the scope of paragraph 4 (a) of this Article tend, when they are in rapid process of development, to experience balance of payments difficulties arising mainly from efforts to expand their internal markets as well as from the instability in their terms of trade.

9.   In order to safeguard its external financial position and to ensure a level of reserves adequate for the implementation of its programme of economic development, a contracting party coming within the scope of paragraph 4 (*a*) of this Article may, subject to the provisions of paragraphs 10 to 12, control the general level of its imports by restricting the quantity or value of merchandise permitted to be imported; *Provided* that the import restrictions instituted, maintained or intensified shall not exceed those necessary:

(*a*) to forestall the threat of, or to stop, a serious decline in its monetary reserves, or

(*b*) in the case of a contracting party with inadequate monetary reserves, to achieve a reasonable rate of increase in its reserves.

Due regard shall be paid in either case to any special factors which may be affecting the reserves of the contracting party or its need for reserves, including, where special external credits or other resources are available to it, the need to provide for the appropriate use of such credits or resources.

10.   In applying these restrictions, the contracting party may determine their incidence on imports of different products or classes of products in such a way as to give priority to the importation of those products which are more essential in the light of its policy of economic development; *Provided* that the restrictions are so applied as to avoid unnecessary damage to the commercial or economic interests of any other contracting party and not to prevent unreasonably the importation of any description of goods in minimum commercial quantities the exclusion of which would impair regular channels of trade; and *Provided* further that the restrictions are not so applied as to prevent the importation of commercial samples or to prevent compliance with patent, trade mark, copyright or similar procedures.

11.   In carrying out its domestic policies, the contracting party concerned shall pay due regard to the need for restoring equilibrium in its balance of payments on a sound and lasting basis and to the desirability of assuring an economic employment of productive resources. It shall progressively relax any restrictions applied under this Section as conditions improve, maintaining them only to the extent necessary under the terms of paragraph 9 of this Article and shall eliminate them when conditions no longer justify such maintenance; *Provided* that no contracting party shall be required to withdraw or modify restrictions on the ground that a change in its development policy would render unnecessary the restrictions which it is applying under this Section.*

12.   (*a*) Any contracting party applying new restrictions or raising the general level of its existing restrictions by a substantial intensification

of the measures applied under this Section, shall immediately after instituting or intensifying such restrictions (or, in circumstances in which prior consultation is practicable, before doing so) consult with the CONTRACTING PARTIES as to the nature of its balance of payments difficulties, alternative corrective measures which may be available, and the possible effect of the restrictions on the economies of other contracting parties.

(b) On a date to be determined by them,* the CONTRACTING PARTIES shall review all restrictions still applied under this Section on that date. Beginning two years after that date, contracting parties applying restrictions under this Section shall enter into consultations of the type provided for in sub-paragraph (a) above with the CONTRACTING PARTIES at intervals of approximately, but not less than, two years according to a programme to be drawn up each year by the CONTRACTING PARTIES; *Provided* that no consultation under this sub-paragraph shall take place within two years after the conclusion of a consultation of a general nature under any other provision of this paragraph.

(c) (i) If, in the course of consultations with a contracting party under sub-paragraph (a) or (b) of this paragraph, the CONTRACTING PARTIES find that the restrictions are not consistent with the provisions of this Section or with those of Article XIII (subject to the provisions of Article XIV), they shall indicate the nature of the inconsistency and may advise that the restrictions be suitably modified.

(ii) If, however, as a result of the consultations, the CONTRACTING PARTIES determine that the restrictions are being applied in a manner involving an inconsistency of a serious nature with the provisions of this Section or with those of Article XIII (subject to the provisions of Article XIV) and that damage to the trade of any contracting party is caused or threatened thereby, they shall so inform the contracting party applying the restrictions and shall make appropriate recommendations for securing conformity with such provisions within a specified period. If such contracting party does not comply with these recommendations within the specified period, the CONTRACTING PARTIES may release any contracting party the trade of which is adversely affected by the restrictions from such obligations under this Agreement towards the contracting party applying the restrictions as they determine to be appropriate in the circumstances.

(d) The CONTRACTING PARTIES shall invite any contracting party which is applying restrictions under this Section to enter into consultations with them at the request of any contracting party which can establish a *prima facie* case that the restrictions are inconsistent with the provisions of this Section or with those of Article XIII (subject to the provisions of Article XIV) and that its trade is adversely affected thereby. However, no such invitation shall be issued unless the CONTRACTING PARTIES have ascertained that direct discussions between the contracting parties concerned have not been successful. If, as a result of the consultations with the CONTRACTING PARTIES no agreement is reached and they determine that the restrictions are being applied inconsistently with such provisions, and that damage to the trade of the contracting party initiating the procedure is caused or threatened thereby, they shall recommend the withdrawal or modification of the restrictions. If the restrictions are not withdrawn or modified within such time as the CONTRACTING PARTIES may prescribe, they may release the contracting party initiating the procedure from such obligations under this Agreement towards the contracting party applying the restrictions as they determine to be appropriate in the circumstances.

(e) If a contracting party against which action has been taken in accordance with the last sentence of sub-paragraph (c) (ii) or (d) of this paragraph, finds that the release of obligations authorized by the CON-TRACTING PARTIES adversely affects the operation of its programme and policy of economic development, it shall be free, not later than sixty days after such action is taken, to give written notice to the Executive Secretary [1] to the CONTRACTING PARTIES of its intention to withdraw from this Agreement and such withdrawal shall take effect on the sixtieth day following the day on which the notice is received by him.

(f) In proceeding under this paragraph, the CONTRACTING PARTIES shall have due regard to the factors referred to in paragraph 2 of this Article. Determinations under this paragraph shall be rendered expeditiously and, if possible, within sixty days of the initiation of the consultations.

Section C

13. If a contracting party coming within the scope of paragraph 4 (a) of this Article finds that governmental assistance is required to promote the establishment of a particular industry * with a view to raising the general standard of living of its people, but that no measure consistent with the other provisions of this Agreement is practicable to achieve that objective, it may have recourse to the provisions and procedures set out in this Section.*

14. The contracting party concerned shall notify the CONTRACTING PARTIES of the special difficulties which it meets in the achievement of the objective outlined in paragraph 13 of this Article and shall indicate the specific measure affecting imports which it proposes to introduce in order to remedy these difficulties. It shall not introduce that measure before the expiration of the time-limit laid down in paragraph 15 or 17, as the case may be, or if the measure affects imports of a product which is the subject of a concession included in the appropriate Schedule annexed to

---

[1] See Preface.

this Agreement, unless it has secured the concurrence of the CONTRACTING PARTIES in accordance with the provisions of paragraph 18; *Provided* that, if the industry receiving assistance has already started production, the contracting party may, after informing the CONTRACTING PARTIES, take such measures as may be necessary to prevent, during that period, imports of the product or products concerned from increasing substantially above a normal level.*

15. If, within thirty days of the notification of the measure, the CONTRACTING PARTIES do not request the contracting party concerned to consult with them,* that contracting party shall be free to deviate from the relevant provisions of the other Articles of this Agreement to the extent necessary to apply the proposed measure.

16. If it is requested by the CONTRACTING PARTIES to do so,* the contracting party concerned shall consult with them as to the purpose of the proposed measure, as to alternative measures which may be available under this Agreement, and as to the possible effect of the measure proposed on the commercial and economic interests of other contracting parties. If, as a result of such consultation, the CONTRACTING PARTIES agree that there is no measure consistent with the other provisions of this Agreement which is practicable in order to achieve the objective outlined in paragraph 13 of this Article, and concur * in the proposed measure, the contracting party concerned shall be released from its obligations under the relevant provisions of the other Articles of this Agreement to the extent necessary to apply that measure.

17. If, within ninety days after the date of the notification of the proposed measure under paragraph 14 of this Article, the CONTRACTING PARTIES have not concurred in such measure, the contracting party concerned may introduce the measure proposed after informing the CONTRACTING PARTIES.

18. If the proposed measure affects a product which is the subject of a concession included in the appropriate Schedule annexed to this Agreement, the contracting party concerned shall enter into consultations with any other contracting party with which the concession was initially negotiated, and with any other contracting party determined by the CONTRACTING PARTIES to have a substantial interest therein. The CONTRACTING PARTIES shall concur * in the measure if they agree that there is no measure consistent with the other provisions of this Agreement which is practicable in order to achieve the objective set forth in paragraph 13 of this Article, and if they are satisfied:

(*a*) that agreement has been reached with such other contracting parties as a result of the consultations referred to above, or

132

(*b*) if no such agreement has been reached within sixty days after the notification provided for in paragraph 14 has been received by the CONTRACTING PARTIES, that the contracting party having recourse to this Section has made all reasonable efforts to reach an agreement and that the interests of other contracting parties are adequately safeguarded.*

The contracting party having recourse to this Section shall thereupon be released from its obligations under the relevant provisions of the other Articles of this Agreement to the extent necessary to permit it to apply the measure.

19.   If a proposed measure of the type described in paragraph 13 of this Article concerns an industry the establishment of which has in the initial period been facilitated by incidental protection afforded by restrictions imposed by the contracting party concerned for balance of payments purposes under the relevant provisions of this Agreement, that contracting party may resort to the provisions and procedures of this Section; *Provided* that it shall not apply the proposed measure without the concurrence * of the CONTRACTING PARTIES.*

20.   Nothing in the preceding paragraphs of this Section shall authorize any deviation from the provisions of Articles I, II and XIII of this Agreement.   The provisos to paragraph 10 of this Article shall also be applicable to any restriction under this Section.

21.   At any time while a measure is being applied under paragraph 17 of this Article any contracting party substantially affected by it may suspend the application to the trade of the contracting party having recourse to this Section of such substantially equivalent concessions or other obligations under this Agreement the suspension of which the CONTRACTING PARTIES do not disapprove; * *Provided* that sixty days' notice of such suspension is given to the CONTRACTING PARTIES not later than six months after the measure has been introduced or changed substantially to the detriment of the contracting party affected.   Any such contracting party shall afford adequate opportunity for consultation in accordance with the provisions of Article XXII of this Agreement.

Section D

22.   A contracting party coming within the scope of sub-paragraph 4 (*b*) of this Article desiring, in the interest of the development of its economy, to introduce a measure of the type described in paragraph 13 of this Article in respect of the establishment of a particular industry * may apply to the CONTRACTING PARTIES for approval of such measure.   The CONTRACTING PARTIES shall promptly consult with such contracting party

and shall, in making their decision, be guided by the considerations set out in paragraph 16. If the CONTRACTING PARTIES concur * in the proposed measure the contracting party concerned shall be released from its obligations under the relevant provisions of the other Articles of this Agreement to the extent necessary to permit it to apply the measure. If the proposed measure affects a product which is the subject of a concession included in the appropriate Schedule annexed to this Agreement, the provisions of paragraph 18 shall apply.*

23. Any measure applied under this Section shall comply with the provisions of paragraph 20 of this Article.

Article XIX

Emergency Action on Imports of Particular Products

1. (*a*) If, as a result of unforeseen developments and of the effect of the obligations incurred by a contracting party under this Agreement, including tariff concessions, any product is being imported into the territory of that contracting party in such increased quantities and under such conditions as to cause or threaten serious injury to domestic producers in that territory of like or directly competitive products, the contracting party shall be free, in respect of such product, and to the extent and for such time as may be necessary to prevent or remedy such injury, to suspend the obligation in whole or in part or to withdraw or modify the concession.

(*b*) If any product, which is the subject of a concession with respect to a preference, is being imported into the territory of a contracting party in the circumstances set forth in sub-paragraph (*a*) of this paragraph, so as to cause or threaten serious injury to domestic producers of like or directly competitive products in the territory of a contracting party which receives or received such preference, the importing contracting party shall be free, if that other contracting party so requests, to suspend the relevant obligation in whole or in part or to withdraw or modify the concession in respect of the product, to the extent and for such time as may be necessary to prevent or remedy such injury.

2. Before any contracting party shall take action pursuant to the provisions of paragraph 1 of this Article, it shall give notice in writing to the CONTRACTING PARTIES as far in advance as may be practicable and shall afford the CONTRACTING PARTIES and those contracting parties having a substantial interest as exporters of the product concerned an opportunity to consult with it in respect of the proposed action. When such notice is given in relation to a concession with respect to a preference, the notice

shall name the contracting party which has requested the action. In critical circumstances, where delay would cause damage which it would be difficult to repair, action under paragraph 1 of this Article may be taken provisionally without prior consultation, on the condition that consultation shall be effected immediately after taking such action.

3. (a) If agreement among the interested contracting parties with respect to the action is not reached, the contracting party which proposes to take or continue the action shall, nevertheless, be free to do so, and if such action is taken or continued, the affected contracting parties shall then be free, not later than ninety days after such action is taken, to suspend, upon the expiration of thirty days from the day on which written notice of such suspension is received by the CONTRACTING PARTIES, the application to the trade of the contracting party taking such action, or, in the case envisaged in paragraph 1 (b) of this Article, to the trade of the contracting party requesting such action, of such substantially equivalent concessions or other obligations under this Agreement the suspension of which the CONTRACTING PARTIES do not disapprove.

(b) Notwithstanding the provisions of sub-paragraph (a) of this paragraph, where action is taken under paragraph 2 of this Article without prior consultation and causes or threatens serious injury in the territory of a contracting party to the domestic producers of products affected by the action, that contracting party shall, where delay would cause damage difficult to repair, be free to suspend, upon the taking of the action and throughout the period of consultation, such concessions or other obligations as may be necessary to prevent or remedy the injury.

Article XX

General Exceptions

Subject to the requirement that such measures are not applied in a manner which would constitute a means of arbitrary or unjustifiable discrimination between countries where the same conditions prevail, or a disguised restriction on international trade, nothing in this Agreement shall be construed to prevent the adoption or enforcement by any contracting party of measures:

(a) necessary to protect public morals;

(b) necessary to protect human, animal or plant life or health;

(c) relating to the importation or exportation of gold or silver;

(d) necessary to secure compliance with laws or regulations which are not inconsistent with the provisions of this Agreement, including those relating to customs enforcement, the enforcement of monopolies operated under paragraph 4 of Article II and Article XVII, the protection of patents, trade marks and copyrights, and the prevention of deceptive practices;

(e) relating to the products of prison labour;

(f) imposed for the protection of national treasures of artistic, historic or archaeological value;

(g) relating to the conservation of exhaustible natural resources if such measures are made effective in conjunction with restrictions on domestic production or consumption;

(h) undertaken in pursuance of obligations under any intergovernmental commodity agreement which conforms to criteria submitted to the CONTRACTING PARTIES and not disapproved by them or which is itself so submitted and not so disapproved;*

(i) involving restrictions on exports of domestic materials necessary to ensure essential quantities of such materials to a domestic processing industry during periods when the domestic price of such materials is held below the world price as part of a governmental stabilization plan; *Provided* that such restrictions shall not operate to increase the exports of or the protection afforded to such domestic industry, and shall not depart from the provisions of this Agreement relating to non-discrimination;

(j) essential to the acquisition or distribution of products in general or local short supply; *Provided* that any such measures shall be consistent with the principle that all contracting parties are entitled to an equitable share of the international supply of such products, and that any such measures, which are inconsistent with the other provisions of this Agreement shall be discontinued as soon as the conditions giving rise to them have ceased to exist. The CONTRACTING PARTIES shall review the need for this sub-paragraph not later than 30 June 1960.

Article XXI

Security Exceptions

Nothing in this Agreement shall be construed

(a) to require any contracting party to furnish any information the disclosure of which it considers contrary to its essential security interests; or (*b*) to prevent any contracting party from taking any action which it considers necessary for the protection of its essential security interests

    (i) relating to fissionable materials or the materials from which they are derived;

    (ii) relating to the traffic in arms, ammunition and implements of war and to such traffic in other goods and materials as is carried on directly or indirectly for the purpose of supplying a military establishment;

    (iii) taken in time of war or other emergency in international relations; or

(*c*) to prevent any contracting party from taking any action in pursuance of its obligations under the United Nations Charter for the maintenance of international peace and security.

Article XXII

Consultation

1. Each contracting party shall accord sympathetic consideration to, and shall afford adequate opportunity for consultation regarding, such representations as may be made by another contracting party with respect to any matter affecting the operation of this Agreement.

2. The CONTRACTING PARTIES may, at the request of a contracting party, consult with any contracting party or parties in respect of any matter for which it has not been possible to find a satisfactory solution through consultation under paragraph 1.

Article XXIII

Nullification or Impairment

1. If any contracting party should consider that any benefit accruing to it directly or indirectly under this Agreement is being nullified or impaired or that the attainment of any objective of the Agreement is being impeded as the result of

(*a*) the failure of another contracting party to carry out its obligations under this Agreement, or

(*b*) the application by another contracting party of any measure, whether or not it conflicts with the provisions of this Agreement, or

(*c*) the existence of any other situation,

137

the contracting party may, with a view to the satisfactory adjustment of the matter, make written representations or proposals to the other contracting party or parties which it considers to be concerned. Any contracting party thus approached shall give sympathetic consideration to the representations or proposals made to it.

2. If no satisfactory adjustment is effected between the contracting parties concerned within a reasonable time, or if the difficulty is of the type described in paragraph 1 (*c*) of this Article, the matter may be referred to the CONTRACTING PARTIES. The CONTRACTING PARTIES shall promptly investigate any matter so referred to them and shall make appropriate recommendations to the contracting parties which they consider to be concerned, or give a ruling on the matter, as appropriate. The CONTRACTING PARTIES may consult with contracting parties, with the Economic and Social Council of the United Nations and with any appropriate inter-governmental organization in cases where they consider such consultation necessary. If the CONTRACTING PARTIES consider that the circumstances are serious enough to justify such action, they may authorize a contracting party or parties to suspend the application to any other contracting party or parties of such concessions or other obligations under this Agreement as they determine to be appropriate in the circumstances. If the application to any contracting party of any concession or other obligation is in fact suspended, that contracting party shall then be free, not later than sixty days after such action is taken, to give written notice to the Executive Secretary[1] to the CONTRACTING PARTIES of its intention to withdraw from this Agreement and such withdrawal shall take effect upon the sixtieth day following the day on which such notice is received by him.

---

[1] See Preface.

138

PART III

Article XXIV

Territorial Application—Frontier Traffic—Customs Unions and Free-trade Areas

1. The provisions of this Agreement shall apply to the metropolitan customs territories of the contracting parties and to any other customs territories in respect of which this Agreement has been accepted under Article XXVI or is being applied under Article XXXIII or pursuant to the Protocol of Provisional Application. Each such customs territory shall, exclusively for the purposes of the territorial application of this Agreement, be treated as though it were a contracting party; *Provided* that the provisions of this paragraph shall not be construed to create any rights or obligations as between two or more customs territories in respect of which this Agreement has been accepted under Article XXVI or is being applied under Article XXXIII or pursuant to the Protocol of Provisional Application by a single contracting party.

2. For the purposes of this Agreement a customs territory shall be understood to mean any territory with respect to which separate tariffs or other regulations of commerce are maintained for a substantial part of the trade of such territory with other territories.

3. The provisions of this Agreement shall not be construed to prevent:

  (*a*) Advantages accorded by any contracting party to adjacent countries in order to facilitate frontier traffic;

  (*b*) Advantages accorded to the trade with the Free Territory of Trieste by countries contiguous to that territory, provided that such advantages are not in conflict with the Treaties of Peace arising out of the Second World War.

4. The contracting parties recognize the desirability of increasing freedom of trade by the development, through voluntary agreements, of closer integration between the economies of the countries parties to such agreements. They also recognize that the purpose of a customs union or of a free-trade area should be to facilitate trade between the constituent territories and not to raise barriers to the trade of other contracting parties with such territories.

5.   Accordingly, the provisions of this Agreement shall not prevent, as between the territories of contracting parties, the formation of a customs union or of a free-trade area or the adoption of an interim agreement necessary for the formation of a customs union or of a free-trade area; *Provided* that:

(*a*)   with respect to a customs union, or an interim agreement leading to the formation of a customs union, the duties and other regulations of commerce imposed at the institution of any such union or interim agreement in respect of trade with contracting parties not parties to such union or agreement shall not on the whole be higher or more restrictive than the general incidence of the duties and regulations of commerce applicable in the constituent territories prior to the formation of such union or the adoption of such interim agreement, as the case may be;

(*b*)   with respect to a free-trade area, or an interim agreement leading to the formation of a free-trade area, the duties and other regulations of commerce maintained in each of the constituent territories and applicable at the formation of such free-trade area or the adoption of such interim agreement to the trade of contracting parties not included in such area or not parties to such agreement shall not be higher or more restrictive than the corresponding duties and other regulations of commerce existing in the same constituent territories prior to the formation of the free-trade area, or interim agreement, as the case may be; and

(*c*)   any interim agreement referred to in sub-paragraphs (*a*) and (*b*) shall include a plan and schedule for the formation of such a customs union or of such a free-trade area within a reasonable length of time.

6.   If, in fulfilling the requirements of sub-paragraph 5 (*a*), a contracting party proposes to increase any rate of duty inconsistently with the provisions of Article II, the procedure set forth in Article XXVIII shall apply. In providing for compensatory adjustment, due account shall be taken of the compensation already afforded by the reductions brought about in the corresponding duty of the other constituents of the union.

7.   (*a*) Any contracting party deciding to enter into a customs union or free-trade area, or an interim agreement leading to the formation of such a union or area, shall promptly notify the CONTRACTING PARTIES and shall make available to them such information regarding the proposed union or area as will enable them to make such reports and recommendations to contracting parties as they may deem appropriate.

(*b*) If, after having studied the plan and schedule included in an interim agreement referred to in paragraph 5 in consultation with the parties to that agreement and taking due account of the information made available in accordance with the provisions of sub-paragraph (*a*), the CONTRACTING PARTIES find that such agreement is not likely to result in the formation of a customs union or of a free-trade area within the period contemplated by the parties to the agreement or that such period is not a reasonable one, the CONTRACTING PARTIES shall make recommendations to the parties to the agreement. The parties shall not maintain or put into force, as the case may be, such agreement if they are not prepared to modify it in accordance with these recommendations.

(*c*) Any substantial change in the plan or schedule referred to in paragraph 5 (*c*) shall be communicated to the CONTRACTING PARTIES, which may request the contracting parties concerned to consult with them if the change seems likely to jeopardize or delay unduly the formation of the customs union or of the free-trade area.

8. For the purposes of this Agreement:

(*a*) A customs union shall be understood to mean the substitution of a single customs territory for two or more customs territories, so that

  (i) duties and other restrictive regulations of commerce (except, where necessary, those permitted under Articles XI, XII, XIII, XIV, XV and XX) are eliminated with respect to substantially all the trade between the constituent territories of the union or at least with respect to substantially all the trade in products originating in such territories, and,

  (ii) subject to the provisions of paragraph 9, substantially the same duties and other regulations of commerce are applied by each of the members of the union to the trade of territories not included in the union;

(*b*) A free-trade area shall be understood to mean a group of two or more customs territories in which the duties and other restrictive regulations of commerce (except, where necessary, those permitted under Articles XI, XII, XIII, XIV, XV and XX) are eliminated on substantially all the trade between the constituent territories in products originating in such territories.

9. The preferences referred to in paragraph 2 of Article I shall not be affected by the formation of a customs union or of a free-trade area but may be eliminated or adjusted by means of negotiations with contracting parties affected.* This procedure of negotiations with affected contracting parties shall, in particular, apply to the elimination of preferences required to conform with the provisions of paragraph 8 (*a*) (i) and paragraph 8 (*b*).

141

10.   The CONTRACTING PARTIES may by a two-thirds majority approve proposals which do not fully comply with the requirements of paragraphs 5 to 9 inclusive, provided that such proposals lead to the formation of a customs union or a free-trade area in the sense of this Article.

11.   Taking into account the exceptional circumstances arising out of the establishment of India and Pakistan as independent States and recognizing the fact that they have long constituted an economic unit, the contracting parties agree that the provisions of this Agreement shall not prevent the two countries from entering into special arrangements with respect to the trade between them, pending the establishment of their mutual trade relations on a definitive basis.*

12.   Each contracting party shall take such reasonable measures as may be available to it to ensure observance of the provisions of this Agreement by the regional and local governments and authorities within its territory.

Article XXV

Joint Action by the Contracting Parties

1.   Representatives of the contracting parties shall meet from time to time for the purpose of giving effect to those provisions of this Agreement which involve joint action and, generally, with a view to facilitating the operation and furthering the objectives of this Agreement. Wherever reference is made in this Agreement to the contracting parties acting jointly they are designated as the CONTRACTING PARTIES.

2.   The Secretary-General of the United Nations is requested to convene the first meeting of the CONTRACTING PARTIES, which shall take place not later than March 1, 1948.

3.   Each contracting party shall be entitled to have one vote at all meetings of the CONTRACTING PARTIES.

4.   Except as otherwise provided for in this Agreement, decisions of the CONTRACTING PARTIES shall be taken by a majority of the votes cast.

5.   In exceptional circumstances not elsewhere provided for in this Agreement, the CONTRACTING PARTIES may waive an obligation imposed upon a contracting party by this Agreement; *Provided* that any such decision shall be approved by a two-thirds majority of the votes cast and that such majority shall comprise more than half of the contracting parties. The CONTRACTING PARTIES may also by such a vote

(i) define certain categories of exceptional circumstances to which other voting requirements shall apply for the waiver of obligations, and

(ii) prescribe such criteria as may be necessary for the application of this paragraph.†

Article XXVI

Acceptance, Entry into Force and Registration

1. The date of this Agreement shall be 30 October 1947.

2. This Agreement shall be open for acceptance by any contracting party which, on 1 March 1955, was a contracting party or was negotiating with a view to accession to this Agreement.

3. This Agreement, done in a single English original and in a single French original, both texts authentic, shall be deposited with the Secretary-General of the United Nations, who shall furnish certified copies thereof to all interested governments.

4. Each government accepting this Agreement shall deposit an instrument of acceptance with the Executive Secretary[1] to the CONTRACTING PARTIES, who will inform all interested governments of the date of deposit of each instrument of acceptance and of the day on which this Agreement enters into force under paragraph 6 of this Article.

5. (*a*) Each government accepting this Agreement does so in respect of its metropolitan territory and of the other territories for which it has international responsibility, except such separate customs territories as it shall notify to the Executive Secretary[1] to the CONTRACTING PARTIES at the time of its own acceptance.

(*b*) Any government, which has so notified the Executive Secretary[1] under the exceptions in sub-paragraph (*a*) of this paragraph, may at any time give notice to the Executive Secretary[1] that its acceptance shall be effective in respect of any separate customs territory or territories so excepted and such notice shall take effect on the thirtieth day following the day on which it is received by the Executive Secretary.[1]

(*c*) If any of the customs territories, in respect of which a contracting party has accepted this Agreement, possesses or acquires full autonomy in the conduct of its external commercial relations and of the other matters

---

† The authentic text erroneously reads " sub-paragraph ".
[1] See Preface.

provided for in this Agreement, such territory shall, upon sponsorship through a declaration by the responsible contracting party establishing the above-mentioned fact, be deemed to be a contracting party.

6. This Agreement shall enter into force, as among the governments which have accepted it, on the thirtieth day following the day on which instruments of acceptance have been deposited with the Executive Secretary[1] to the CONTRACTING PARTIES on behalf of governments named in Annex H, the territories of which account for 85 per centum of the total external trade of the territories of such governments, computed in accordance with the applicable column of percentages set forth therein. The instrument of acceptance of each other government shall take effect on the thirtieth day following the day on which such instrument has been deposited.

7. The United Nations is authorized to effect registration of this Agreement as soon as it enters into force.

Article XXVII

Withholding or Withdrawal of Concessions

Any contracting party shall at any time be free to withhold or to withdraw in whole or in part any concession, provided for in the appropriate Schedule annexed to this Agreement, in respect of which such contracting party determines that it was initially negotiated with a government which has not become, or has ceased to be, a contracting party. A contracting party taking such action shall notify the CONTRACTING PARTIES and, upon request, consult with contracting parties which have a substantial interest in the product concerned.

Article XXVIII *

Modification of Schedules

1. On the first day of each three-year period, the first period beginning on 1 January 1958 (or on the first day of any other period * that may be specified by the CONTRACTING PARTIES by two-thirds of the votes cast) a contracting party (hereafter in this Article referred to as the "applicant contracting party") may, by negotiation and agreement with any contracting party with which such concession was initially negotiated and with any other contracting party determined by the CONTRACTING PARTIES to have a principal supplying interest* (which two preceding categories of contracting

---

[1] See Preface.

parties, together with the applicant contracting party, are in this Article hereinafter referred to as the "contracting parties primarily concerned"), and subject to consultation with any other contracting party determined by the CONTRACTING PARTIES to have a substantial interest* in such concession, modify or withdraw a concession* included in the appropriate Schedule annexed to this Agreement.

2. In such negotiations and agreement, which may include provision for compensatory adjustment with respect to other products, the contracting parties concerned shall endeavour to maintain a general level of reciprocal and mutually advantageous concessions not less favourable to trade than that provided for in this Agreement prior to such negotiations.

3. (a) If agreement between the contracting parties primarily concerned cannot be reached before 1 January 1958 or before the expiration of a period envisaged in paragraph 1 of this Article, the contracting party which proposes to modify or withdraw the concession shall, nevertheless, be free to do so and if such action is taken any contracting party with which such concession was initially negotiated, any contracting party determined under paragraph 1 to have a principal supplying interest and any contracting party determined under paragraph 1 to have a substantial interest shall then be free not later than six months after such action is taken, to withdraw, upon the expiration of thirty days from the day on which written notice of such withdrawal is received by the CONTRACTING PARTIES, substantially equivalent concessions initially negotiated with the applicant contracting party.

(b) If agreement between the contracting parties primarily concerned is reached but any other contracting party determined under paragraph 1 of this Article to have a substantial interest is not satisfied, such other contracting party shall be free, not later than six months after action under such agreement is taken, to withdraw, upon the expiration of thirty days from the day on which written notice of such withdrawal is received by the CONTRACTING PARTIES, substantially equivalent concessions initially negotiated with the applicant contracting party.

4. The CONTRACTING PARTIES may, at any time, in special circumstances, authorize* a contracting party to enter into negotiations for modification or withdrawal of a concession included in the appropriate Schedule annexed to this Agreement subject to the following procedures and conditions:

(a) Such negotiations* and any related consultations shall be conducted in accordance with the provisions of paragraphs 1 and 2 of this Article.

(b) If agreement between the contracting parties primarily concerned is reached in the negotiations, the provisions of paragraph 3 (b) of this Article shall apply.

(c) If agreement between the contracting parties primarily concerned is not reached within a period of sixty days* after negotiations have been authorized, or within such longer period as the CONTRACTING PARTIES may have prescribed, the applicant contracting party may refer the matter to the CONTRACTING PARTIES.

(d) Upon such reference, the CONTRACTING PARTIES shall promptly examine the matter and submit their views to the contracting parties primarily concerned with the aim of achieving a settlement. If a settlement is reached, the provisions of paragraph 3 (b) shall apply as if agreement between the contracting parties primarily concerned had been reached. If no settlement is reached between the contracting parties primarily concerned, the applicant contracting party shall be free to modify or withdraw the concession, unless the CONTRACTING PARTIES determine that the applicant contracting party has unreasonably failed to offer adequate compensation.* If such action is taken, any contracting party with which the concession was initially negotiated, any contracting party determined under paragraph 4 (a) to have a principal supplying interest and any contracting party determined under paragraph 4 (a) to have a substantial interest, shall be free, not later than six months after such action is taken, to modify or withdraw, upon the expiration of thirty days from the day on which written notice of such withdrawal is received by the CONTRACTING PARTIES, substantially equivalent concessions initially negotiated with the applicant contracting party.

5. Before 1 January 1958 and before the end of any period envisaged in paragraph 1 a contracting party may elect by notifying the CONTRACTING PARTIES to reserve the right, for the duration of the next period, to modify the appropriate Schedule in accordance with the procedures of paragraphs 1 to 3. If a contracting party so elects, other contracting parties shall have the right, during the same period, to modify or withdraw, in accordance with the same procedures, concessions initially negotiated with that contracting party.

Article XXVIII bis

Tariff Negotiations

1. The contracting parties recognize that customs duties often constitute serious obstacles to trade; thus negotiations on a reciprocal and mutually advantageous basis, directed to the substantial reduction of the general level of tariffs and other charges on imports and exports and in particular to the reduction of such high tariffs as discourage the importation even of minimum quantities, and conducted with due regard to the objectives of this Agreement

146

and the varying needs of individual contracting parties, are of great importance to the expansion of international trade. The CONTRACTING PARTIES may therefore sponsor such negotiations from time to time.

2. (*a*) Negotiations under this Article may be carried out on a selective product-by-product basis or by the application of such multilateral procedures as may be accepted by the contracting parties concerned. Such negotiations may be directed towards the reduction of duties, the binding of duties at then existing levels or undertakings that individual duties or the average duties on specified categories of products shall not exceed specified levels. The binding against increase of low duties or of duty-free treatment shall, in principle, be recognized as a concession equivalent in value to the reduction of high duties.

(*b*) The contracting parties recognize that in general the success of multilateral negotiations would depend on the participation of all contracting parties which conduct a substantial proportion of their external trade with one another.

3. Negotiations shall be conducted on a basis which affords adequate opportunity to take into account:

(*a*) the needs of individual contracting parties and individual industries;

(*b*) the needs of less-developed countries for a more flexible use of tariff protection to assist their economic development and the special needs of these countries to maintain tariffs for revenue purposes; and

(*c*) all other relevant circumstances, including the fiscal,* developmental, strategic and other needs of the contracting parties concerned.

Article XXIX

The Relation of this Agreement to the Havana Charter

1. The contracting parties undertake to observe to the fullest extent of their executive authority the general principles of Chapters I to VI inclusive and of Chapter IX of the Havana Charter pending their acceptance of it in accordance with their constitutional procedures.*

2. Part II of this Agreement shall be suspended on the day on which the Havana Charter enters into force.

3. If by September 30, 1949, the Havana Charter has not entered into force, the contracting parties shall meet before December 31, 1949, to agree whether this Agreement shall be amended, supplemented or maintained.

4. If at any time the Havana Charter should cease to be in force, the CONTRACTING PARTIES shall meet as soon as practicable thereafter to agree whether this Agreement shall be supplemented, amended or maintained. Pending such agreement, Part II of this Agreement shall again enter into force; *Provided* that the provisions of Part II other than Article XXIII shall be replaced, *mutatis mutandis*, in the form in which they then appeared in the Havana Charter; and *Provided* further that no contracting party shall be bound by any provisions which did not bind it at the time when the Havana Charter ceased to be in force.

5. If any contracting party has not accepted the Havana Charter by the date upon which it enters into force, the CONTRACTING PARTIES shall confer to agree whether, and if so in what way, this Agreement in so far as it affects relations between such contracting party and other contracting parties, shall be supplemented or amended. Pending such agreement the provisions of Part II of this Agreement shall, notwithstanding the provisions of paragraph 2 of this Article, continue to apply as between such contracting party and other contracting parties.

6. Contracting parties which are Members of the International Trade Organization shall not invoke the provisions of this Agreement so as to prevent the operation of any provision of the Havana Charter. The application of the principle underlying this paragraph to any contracting party which is not a Member of the International Trade Organization shall be the subject of an agreement pursuant to paragraph 5 of this Article.

Article XXX

Amendments

1. Except where provision for modification is made elsewhere in this Agreement, amendments to the provisions of Part I of this Agreement or to the provisions of Article XXIX or of this Article shall become effective upon acceptance by all the contracting parties, and other amendments to this Agreement shall become effective, in respect of those contracting parties which accept them, upon acceptance by two-thirds of the contracting parties and thereafter for each other contracting party upon acceptance by it.

2. Any contracting party accepting an amendment to this Agreement shall deposit an instrument of acceptance with the Secretary-General of the United Nations within such period as the CONTRACTING PARTIES may specify. The CONTRACTING PARTIES may decide that any amendment made effective under this Article is of such a nature that any contracting party

which has not accepted it within a period specified by the CONTRACTING PARTIES shall be free to withdraw from this Agreement, or to remain a contracting party with the consent of the CONTRACTING PARTIES.

Article XXXI

Withdrawal

Without prejudice to the provisions of paragraph 12 of Article XVIII, of Article XXIII or of paragraph 2 of Article XXX, any contracting party may withdraw from this Agreement, or may separately withdraw on behalf of any of the separate customs territories for which it has international responsibility and which at the time possesses full autonomy in the conduct of its external commercial relations and of the other matters provided for in this Agreement. The withdrawal shall take effect upon the expiration of six months from the day on which written notice of withdrawal is received by the Secretary-General of the United Nations.

Article XXXII

Contracting Parties

1. The contracting parties to this Agreement shall be understood to mean those governments which are applying the provisions of this Agreement under Articles XXVI or XXXIII or pursuant to the Protocol of Provisional Application.

2. At any time after the entry into force of this Agreement pursuant to paragraph 6 of Article XXVI, those contracting parties which have accepted this Agreement pursuant to paragraph 4 of Article XXVI may decide that any contracting party which has not so accepted it shall cease to be a contracting party.

Article XXXIII

Accession

A government not party to this Agreement, or a government acting on behalf of a separate customs territory possessing full autonomy in the conduct of its external commercial relations and of the other matters provided for in this Agreement, may accede to this Agreement, on its own behalf or on behalf of that territory, on terms to be agreed between such government and the CONTRACTING PARTIES. Decisions of the CONTRACTING PARTIES under this paragraph shall be taken by a two-thirds majority.

Article XXXIV

Annexes

The annexes to this Agreement are hereby made an integral part of this Agreement.

Article XXXV

*Non-application of the Agreement between
particular Contracting Parties*

1.   This Agreement, or alternatively Article II of this Agreement, shall not apply as between any contracting party and any other contracting party if:

(*a*)   the two contracting parties have not entered into tariff negotiations with each other, and

(*b*)   either of the contracting parties, at the time either becomes a contracting party, does not consent to such application.

2.   The CONTRACTING PARTIES may review the operation of this Article in particular cases at the request of any contracting party and make appropriate recommendations.

PART IV *

TRADE AND DEVELOPMENT

Article XXXVI

Principles and Objectives

1.* The contracting parties,

(*a*) recalling that the basic objectives of this Agreement include the raising of standards of living and the progressive development of the economies of all contracting parties, and considering that the attainment of these objectives is particularly urgent for less-developed contracting parties;

(*b*) considering that export earnings of the less-developed contracting parties can play a vital part in their economic development and that the extent of this contribution depends on the prices paid by the less-developed contracting parties for essential imports, the volume of their exports, and the prices received for these exports;

(*c*) noting, that there is a wide gap between standards of living in less-developed countries and in other countries;

(*d*) recognizing that individual and joint action is essential to further the development of the economies of less-developed contracting parties and to bring about a rapid advance in the standards of living in these countries;

(*e*) recognizing that international trade as a means of achieving economic and social advancement should be governed by such rules and procedures—and measures in conformity with such rules and procedures—as are consistent with the objectives set forth in this Article;

(*f*) noting that the CONTRACTING PARTIES may enable less-developed contracting parties to use special measures to promote their trade and development;

agree as follows.

2. There is need for a rapid and sustained expansion of the export earnings of the less-developed contracting parties.

3. There is need for positive efforts designed to ensure that less-developed contracting parties secure a share in the growth in international trade commensurate with the needs of their economic development.

4. Given the continued dependence of many less-developed contracting parties on the exportation of a limited range of primary products,* there is need to provide in the largest possible measure more favourable and acceptable conditions of access to world markets for these products, and wherever appropriate to devise measures designed to stabilize and improve conditions of world markets in these products, including in particular measures designed to attain stable, equitable and remunerative prices, thus permitting an expansion of world trade and demand and a dynamic and steady growth of the real export earnings of these countries so as to provide them with expanding resources for their economic development.

5. The rapid expansion of the economies of the less-developed contracting parties will be facilitated by a diversification * of the structure of their economies and the avoidance of an excessive dependence on the export of primary products. There is, therefore, need for increased access in the largest possible measure to markets under favourable conditions for processed and manufactured products currently or potentially of particular export interest to less-developed contracting parties.

6. Because of the chronic deficiency in the export proceeds and other foreign exchange earnings of less-developed contracting parties, there are important inter-relationships between trade and financial assistance to development. There is, therefore, need for close and continuing collaboration between the CONTRACTING PARTIES and the international lending agencies so that they can contribute most effectively to alleviating the burdens these less-developed contracting parties assume in the interest of their economic development.

7. There is need for appropriate collaboration between the CONTRACTING PARTIES, other intergovernmental bodies and the organs and agencies of the United Nations system, whose activities relate to the trade and economic development of less-developed countries.

8. The developed contracting parties do not expect reciprocity for commitments made by them in trade negotiations to reduce or remove tariffs and other barriers to the trade of less-developed contracting parties.*

9. The adoption of measures to give effect to these principles and objectives shall be a matter of conscious and purposeful effort on the part of the contracting parties both individually and jointly.

152

Article XXXVII

Commitments

1. The developed contracting parties shall to the fullest extent possible—that is, except when compelling reasons, which may include legal reasons, make it impossible—give effect to the following provisions:

(a) accord high priority to the reduction and elimination of barriers to products currently or potentially of particular export interest to less-developed contracting parties, including customs duties and other restrictions which differentiate unreasonably between such products in their primary and in their processed forms;*

(b) refrain from introducing, or increasing the incidence of, customs duties or non-tariff import barriers on products currently or potentially of particular export interest to less-developed contracting parties; and

(c) (i) refrain from imposing new fiscal measures, and

(ii) in any adjustments of fiscal policy accord high priority to the reduction and elimination of fiscal measures,

which would hamper, or which hamper, significantly the growth of consumption of primary products, in raw or processed form, wholly or mainly produced in the territories of less-developed contracting parties, and which are applied specifically to those products.

2. (a) Whenever it is considered that effect is not being given to any of the provisions of sub-paragraph (a), (b) or (c) of paragraph 1, the matter shall be reported to the CONTRACTING PARTIES either by the contracting party not so giving effect to the relevant provisions or by any other interested contracting party.

(b) (i) The CONTRACTING PARTIES shall, if requested so to do by any interested contracting party, and without prejudice to any bilateral consultations that may be undertaken, consult with the contracting party concerned and all interested contracting parties with respect to the matter with a view to reaching solutions satisfactory to all contracting parties concerned in order to further the objectives set forth in Article XXXVI. In the course of these consultations, the reasons given in cases where effect was not being given to the provisions of sub-paragraph (a), (b) or (c) of paragraph 1 shall be examined.

(ii) As the implementation of the provisions of sub-paragraph (a), (b) or (c) of paragraph 1 by individual contracting parties

153

may in some cases be more readily achieved where action is taken jointly with other developed contracting parties, such consultation might, where appropriate, be directed towards this end.

(iii) The consultations by the CONTRACTING PARTIES might also, in appropriate cases, be directed towards agreement on joint action designed to further the objectives of this Agreement as envisaged in paragraph 1 of Article XXV.

3.   The developed contracting parties shall:

(a)   make every effort, in cases where a government directly or indirectly determines the resale price of products wholly or mainly produced in the territories of less-developed contracting parties, to maintain trade margins at equitable levels;

(b)   give active consideration to the adoption of other measures * designed to provide greater scope for the development of imports from less-developed contracting parties and collaborate in appropriate international action to this end;

(c)   have special regard to the trade interests of less-developed contracting parties when considering the application of other measures permitted under this Agreement to meet particular problems and explore all possibilities of constructive remedies before applying such measures where they would affect essential interests of those contracting parties.

4.   Less-developed contracting parties agree to take appropriate action in implementation of the provisions of Part IV for the benefit of the trade of other less-developed contracting parties, in so far as such action is consistent with their individual present and future development, financial and trade needs taking into account past trade developments as well as the trade interests of less-developed contracting parties as a whole.

5.   In the implementation of the commitments set forth in paragraphs 1 to 4 each contracting party shall afford to any other interested contracting party or contracting parties full and prompt opportunity for consultations under the normal procedures of this Agreement with respect to any matter or difficulty which may arise.

Article XXXVIII

Joint Action

1.   The contracting parties shall collaborate jointly, within the framework of this Agreement and elsewhere, as appropriate, to further the objectives set forth in Article XXXVI.

2. In particular, the CONTRACTING PARTIES shall:

(*a*) where appropriate, take action, including action through international arrangements, to provide improved and acceptable conditions of access to world markets for primary products of particular interest to less-developed contracting parties and to devise measures designed to stabilize and improve conditions of world markets in these products including measures designed to attain stable, equitable and remunerative prices for exports of such products;

(*b*) seek appropriate collaboration in matters of trade and development policy with the United Nations and its organs and agencies, including any institutions that may be created on the basis of recommendations by the United Nations Conference on Trade and Development;

(*c*) collaborate in analysing the development plans and policies of individual less-developed contracting parties and in examining trade and aid relationships with a view to devising concrete measures to promote the development of export potential and to facilitate access to export markets for the products of the industries thus developed and, in this connexion, seek appropriate collaboration with governments and international organizations, and in particular with organizations having competence in relation to financial assistance for economic development, in systematic studies of trade and aid relationships in individual less-developed contracting parties aimed at obtaining a clear analysis of export potential, market prospects and any further action that may be required;

(*d*) keep under continuous review the development of world trade with special reference to the rate of growth of the trade of less-developed contracting parties and make such recommendations to contracting parties as may, in the circumstances, be deemed appropriate;

(*e*) collaborate in seeking feasible methods to expand trade for the purpose of economic development, through international harmonization and adjustment of national policies and regulations, through technical and commercial standards affecting production, transportation and marketing, and through export promotion by the establishment of facilities for the increased flow of trade information and the development of market research; and

(*f*) establish such institutional arrangements as may be necessary to further the objectives set forth in Article XXXVI and to give effect to the provisions of this Part.

ANNEX A

LIST OF TERRITORIES REFERRED TO IN PARAGRAPH 2 (*a*)
OF ARTICLE I

United Kingdom of Great Britain and Northern Ireland
Dependent territories of the United Kingdom of Great Britain and Northern
    Ireland
Canada
Commonwealth of Australia
Dependent territories of the Commonwealth of Australia
New Zealand
Dependent territories of New Zealand
Union of South Africa including South West Africa
Ireland
India (as on April 10, 1947)
Newfoundland
Southern Rhodesia
Burma
Ceylon

   Certain of the territories listed above have two or more preferential rates
in force for certain products. Any such territory may, by agreement with the
other contracting parties which are principal suppliers of such products at the
most-favoured-nation rate, substitute for such preferential rates a single preferential rate which shall not on the whole be less favourable to suppliers at the
most-favoured-nation rate than the preferences in force prior to such substitution.

   The imposition of an equivalent margin of tariff preference to replace a margin
of preference in an internal tax existing on April 10, 1947 exclusively between
two or more of the territories listed in this Annex or to replace the preferential
quantitative arrangements described in the following paragraph, shall not be
deemed to constitute an increase in a margin of tariff preference.

   The preferential arrangements referred to in paragraph 5 (*b*) of Article XIV
are those existing in the United Kingdom on April 10, 1947, under contractual
agreements with the Governments of Canada, Australia and New Zealand, in
respect of chilled and frozen beef and veal, frozen mutton and lamb, chilled and
frozen pork, and bacon. It is the intention, without prejudice to any action taken
under sub-paragraph (*h*) † of Article XX, that these arrangements shall be eliminated or replaced by tariff preferences, and that negotiations to this end shall
take place as soon as practicable among the countries substantially concerned
or involved.

   The film hire tax in force in New Zealand on April 10, 1947, shall, for the
purposes of this Agreement, be treated as a customs duty under Article I. The

---

   † The authentic text erroneously reads " part I (*h*) ".

156

renters' film quota in force in New Zealand on April 10, 1947, shall, for the purposes of this Agreement, be treated as a screen quota under Article IV.

The Dominions of India and Pakistan have not been mentioned separately in the above list since they had not come into existence as such on the base date of April 10, 1947.

ANNEX B

LIST OF TERRITORIES OF THE FRENCH UNION REFERRED TO IN PARAGRAPH 2 (*b*) OF ARTICLE I

France
French Equatorial Africa (Treaty Basin of the Congo [1] and other territories)
French West Africa
Cameroons under French Trusteeship [1]
French Somali Coast and Dependencies
French Establishments in Oceania
French Establishments in the Condominium of the New Hebrides [1]
Indo-China
Madagascar and Dependencies
Morocco (French zone) [1]
New Caledonia and Dependencies
Saint-Pierre and Miquelon
Togo under French Trusteeship [1]
Tunisia

ANNEX C

LIST OF TERRITORIES REFERRED TO IN PARAGRAPH 2 (*b*) OF ARTICLE I AS RESPECTS THE CUSTOMS UNION OF BELGIUM, LUXEMBURG AND THE NETHERLANDS

The Economic Union of Belgium and Luxemburg
Belgian Congo
Ruanda Urundi
Netherlands
New Guinea
Surinam
Netherlands Antilles
Republic of Indonesia

For imports into the territories constituting the Customs Union only.

ANNEX D

LIST OF TERRITORIES REFERRED TO IN PARAGRAPH 2 (*b*) OF ARTICLE I AS RESPECTS THE UNITED STATES OF AMERICA

United States of America (customs territory)
Dependent territories of the United States of America
Republic of the Philippines

---

[1] For imports into Metropolitan France and Territories of the French Union.

The imposition of an equivalent margin of tariff preference to replace a margin of preference in an internal tax existing on April 10, 1947, exclusively between two or more of the territories listed in this Annex shall not be deemed to constitute an increase in a margin of tariff preference.

ANNEX E

LIST OF TERRITORIES COVERED BY PREFERENTIAL ARRANGEMENTS BETWEEN CHILE AND NEIGHBOURING COUNTRIES REFERRED TO IN PARAGRAPH 2 (*d*) OF ARTICLE I

Preferences in force exclusively between Chile on the one hand, and

1. Argentina
2. Bolivia
3. Peru

on the other hand.

ANNEX F

LIST OF TERRITORIES COVERED BY PREFERENTIAL ARRANGEMENTS BETWEEN LEBANON AND SYRIA AND NEIGHBOURING COUNTRIES REFERRED TO IN PARAGRAPH 2 (*d*) OF ARTICLE I

Preferences in force exclusively between the Lebano-Syrian Customs Union, on the one hand, and

1. Palestine
2. Transjordan

on the other hand.

ANNEX G

DATES ESTABLISHING MAXIMUM MARGINS OF PREFERENCE REFERRED TO IN PARAGRAPH 4 † OF ARTICLE I

Australia	October 15, 1946
Canada	July 1, 1939
France	January 1, 1939
Lebano-Syrian Customs Union	November 30, 1938
Union of South Africa	July 1, 1938
Southern Rhodesia	May 1, 1941

ANNEX H

PERCENTAGE SHARES OF TOTAL EXTERNAL TRADE TO BE USED FOR THE PURPOSE OF MAKING THE DETERMINATION REFERRED TO IN ARTICLE XXVI

(based on the average of 1949-1953)

If, prior to the accession of the Government of Japan to the General Agreement, the present Agreement has been accepted by contracting parties the external

---

† The authentic text erroneously reads " Paragraph 3 ".

158

trade of which under column I accounts for the percentage of such trade specified in paragraph 6 of Article XXVI, column I shall be applicable for the purposes of that paragraph. If the present Agreement has not been so accepted prior to the accession of the Government of Japan, column II shall be applicable for the purposes of that paragraph.

	Column I (Contracting parties on 1 March 1955)	Column II (Contracting parties on 1 March 1955 and Japan)
Australia	3.1	3.0
Austria	0.9	0.8
Belgium-Luxemburg	4.3	4.2
Brazil	2.5	2.4
Burma	0.3	0.3
Canada	6.7	6.5
Ceylon	0.5	0.5
Chile	0.6	0.6
Cuba	1.1	1.1
Czechoslovakia	1.4	1.4
Denmark	1.4	1.4
Dominican Republic	0.1	0.1
Finland	1.0	1.0
France	8.7	8.5
Germany, Federal Republic of	5.3	5.2
Greece	0.4	0.4
Haiti	0.1	0.1
India	2.4	2.4
Indonesia	1.3	1.3
Italy	2.9	2.8
Netherlands, Kingdom of the	4.7	4.6
New Zealand	1.0	1.0
Nicaragua	0.1	0.1
Norway	1.1	1.1
Pakistan	0.9	0.8
Peru	0.4	0.4
Rhodesia and Nyasaland	0.6	0.6
Sweden	2.5	2.4
Turkey	0.6	0.6
Union of South Africa	1.8	1.8
United Kingdom	20.3	19.8
United States of America	20.6	20.1
Uruguay	0.4	0.4
Japan	—	2.3
	100.0	100.0

Note: These percentages have been computed taking into account the trade of all territories in respect of which the General Agreement on Tariffs and Trade is applied.

ANNEX I

NOTES AND SUPPLEMENTARY PROVISIONS

Ad *Article I*

Paragraph 1

The obligations incorporated in paragraph 1 of Article I by reference to paragraphs 2 and 4 of Article III and those incorporated in paragraph 2 (*b*) of Article II by reference to Article VI shall be considered as falling within Part II for the purposes of the Protocol of Provisional Application.

The cross-references, in the paragraph immediately above and in paragraph 1 of Article I, to paragraphs 2 and 4 of Article III shall only apply after Article III has been modified by the entry into force of the amendment provided for in the Protocol Modifying Part II and Article XXVI of the General Agreement on Tariffs and Trade, dated September 14, 1948. [1]

Paragraph 4

The term " margin of preference " means the absolute difference between the most-favoured-nation rate of duty and the preferential rate of duty for the like product, and not the proportionate relation between those rates. As examples:

(1) If the most-favoured-nation rate were 36 per cent *ad valorem* and the preferential rate were 24 per cent *ad valorem*, the margin of preference would be 12 per cent *ad valorem*, and not one-third of the most-favoured-nation rate;

(2) If the most-favoured-nation rate were 36 per cent *ad valorem* and the preferential rate were expressed as two-thirds of the most-favoured-nation rate, the margin of preference would be 12 per cent *ad valorem*;

(3) If the most-favoured-nation rate were 2 francs per kilogramme and the preferential rate were 1.50 francs per kilogramme, the margin of preference would be 0.50 franc per kilogramme.

The following kinds of customs action, taken in accordance with established uniform procedures, would not be contrary to a general binding of margins of preference:

(i) The re-application to an imported product of a tariff classification or rate of duty, properly applicable to such product, in cases in which the application of such classification or rate to such product was temporarily suspended or inoperative on April 10, 1947; and

(ii) The classification of a particular product under a tariff item other than that under which importations of that product were classified on April 10, 1947, in cases in which the tariff law clearly contemplates that such product may be classified under more than one tariff item.

---

[1] This Protocol entered into force on 14 December 1948.

Ad *Article II*

Paragraph 2 (a)

The cross-reference, in paragraph 2 (*a*) of Article II, to paragraph 2 of Article III shall only apply after Article III has been modified by the entry into force of the amendment provided for in the Protocol Modifying Part II and Article XXVI of the General Agreement on Tariffs and Trade, dated September 14, 1948. [1]

Paragraph 2 (b)

See the note relating to paragraph 1 of Article I.

Paragraph 4

Except where otherwise specifically agreed between the contracting parties which initially negotiated the concession, the provisions of this paragraph will be applied in the light of the provisions of Article 31 of the Havana Charter.

Ad *Article III*

Any internal tax or other internal charge, or any law, regulation or requirement of the kind referred to in paragraph 1 which applies to an imported product and to the like domestic product and is collected or enforced in the case of the imported product at the time or point of importation, is nevertheless to be regarded as an internal tax or other internal charge, or a law, regulation or requirement of the kind referred to in paragraph 1, and is accordingly subject to the provisions of Article III.

Paragraph 1

The application of paragraph 1 to internal taxes imposed by local governments and authorities within the territory of a contracting party is subject to the provisions of the final paragraph of Article XXIV. The term " reasonable measures " in the last-mentioned paragraph would not require, for example, the repeal of existing national legislation authorizing local governments to impose internal taxes which, although technically inconsistent with the letter of Article III, are not in fact inconsistent with its spirit, if such repeal would result in a serious financial hardship for the local governments or authorities concerned. With regard to taxation by local governments or authorities which is inconsistent with both the letter and spirit of Article III, the term " reasonable measures " would permit a contracting party to eliminate the inconsistent taxation gradually over a transition period, if abrupt action would create serious administrative and financial difficulties.

Paragraph 2

A tax conforming to the requirements of the first sentence of paragraph 2 would be considered to be inconsistent with the provisions of the second sentence

---

[1] This Protocol entered into force on 14 December 1948.

161

only in cases where competition was involved between, on the one hand, the taxed product and, on the other hand, a directly competitive or substitutable product which was not similarly taxed.

Paragraph 5

Regulations consistent with the provisions of the first sentence of paragraph 5 shall not be considered to be contrary to the provisions of the second sentence in any case in which all of the products subject to the regulations are produced domestically in substantial quantities. A regulation cannot be justified as being consistent with the provisions of the second sentence on the ground that the proportion or amount allocated to each of the products which are the subject of the regulation constitutes an equitable relationship between imported and domestic products.

Ad *Article V*

Paragraph 5

With regard to transportation charges, the principle laid down in paragraph 5 refers to like products being transported on the same route under like conditions.

Ad *Article VI*

Paragraph 1

1. Hidden dumping by associated houses (that is, the sale by an importer at a price below that corresponding to the price invoiced by an exporter with whom the importer is associated, and also below the price in the exporting country) constitutes a form of price dumping with respect to which the margin of dumping may be calculated on the basis of the price at which the goods are resold by the importer.

2. It is recognized that, in the case of imports from a country which has a complete or substantially complete monopoly of its trade and where all domestic prices are fixed by the State, special difficulties may exist in determining price comparability for the purposes of paragraph 1, and in such cases importing contracting parties may find it necessary to take into account the possibility that a strict comparison with domestic prices in such a country may not always be appropriate.

Paragraphs 2 and 3

1. As in many other cases in customs administration, a contracting party may require reasonable security (bond or cash deposit) for the payment of anti-dumping or countervailing duty pending final determination of the facts in any case of suspected dumping or subsidization.

2. Multiple currency practices can in certain circumstances constitute a subsidy to exports which may be met by countervailing duties under paragraph 3 or can constitute a form of dumping by means of a partial depreciation of a country's currency which may be met by action under paragraph 2. By " multiple

162

currency practices " is meant practices by governments or sanctioned by governments.

Paragraph 6 (b)

Waivers under the provisions of this sub-paragraph shall be granted only on application by the contracting party proposing to levy an anti-dumping or countervailing duty, as the case may be.

Ad *Article VII*

Paragraph 1

The expression " or other charges " is not to be regarded as including internal taxes or equivalent charges imposed on or in connexion with imported products.

Paragraph 2

1. It would be in conformity with Article VII to presume that " actual value " may be represented by the invoice price, plus any non-included charges for legitimate costs which are proper elements of " actual value " and plus any abnormal discount or other reduction from the ordinary competitive price.

2. It would be in conformity with Article VII, paragraph 2 (*b*), for a contracting party to construe the phrase " in the ordinary course of trade ... under fully competitive conditions ", as excluding any transaction wherein the buyer and seller are not independent of each other and price is not the sole consideration.

3. The standard of " fully competitive conditions " permits a contracting party to exclude from consideration prices involving special discounts limited to exclusive agents.

4. The wording of sub-paragraphs (*a*) and (*b*) permits a contracting party to determine the value for customs purposes uniformly either (1) on the basis of a particular exporter's prices of the imported merchandise, or (2) on the basis of the general price level of like merchandise.

Ad *Article VIII*

1. While Article VIII does not cover the use of multiple rates of exchange as such, paragraphs 1 and 4 condemn the use of exchange taxes or fees as a device for implementing multiple currency practices; if, however, a contracting party is using multiple currency exchange fees for balance of payments reasons with the approval of the International Monetary Fund, the provisions of paragraph 9 (*a*) of Article XV fully safeguard its position.

2. It would be consistent with paragraph 1 if, on the importation of products from the territory of a contracting party into the territory of another contracting party, the production of certificates of origin should only be required to the extent that is strictly indispensable.

Ad *Articles XI, XII, XIII, XIV and XVIII*

Throughout Articles XI, XII, XIII, XIV and XVIII, the terms " import restrictions " or " export restrictions " include restrictions made effective through state-trading operations.

Ad *Article XI*

Paragraph 2 (c)

The term " in any form " in this paragraph covers the same products when in an early stage of processing and still perishable, which compete directly with the fresh product and if freely imported would tend to make the restriction on the fresh product ineffective.

Paragraph 2, last sub-paragraph

The term " special factors " includes changes in relative productive efficiency as between domestic and foreign producers, or as between different foreign producers, but not changes artificially brought about by means not permitted under the Agreement.

Ad *Article XII*

The CONTRACTING PARTIES shall make provision for the utmost secrecy in the conduct of any consultation under the provisions of this Article.

Paragraph 3 (c) (*i*)

Contracting parties applying restrictions shall endeavour to avoid causing serious prejudice to exports of a commodity on which the economy of a contracting party is largely dependent.

Paragraph 4 (b)

It is agreed that the date shall be within ninety days after the entry into force of the amendments of this Article effected by the Protocol Amending the Preamble and Parts II and III of this Agreement. However, should the CONTRACTING PARTIES find that conditions were not suitable for the application of the provisions of this sub-paragraph at the time envisaged, they may determine a later date; *Provided* that such date is not more than thirty days after such time as the obligations of Article VIII, Sections 2, 3 and 4, of the Articles of Agreement of the International Monetary Fund become applicable to contracting parties, members of the Fund, the combined foreign trade of which constitutes at least fifty per centum of the aggregate foreign trade of all contracting parties.

Paragraph 4 (e)

It is agreed that paragraph 4 (*e*) does not add any new criteria for the imposition or maintenance of quantitative restrictions for balance of payments reasons.

164

It is solely intended to ensure that all external factors such as changes in the terms of trade, quantitative restrictions, excessive tariffs and subsidies, which may be contributing to the balance of payments difficulties of the contracting party applying restrictions, will be fully taken into account.

Ad *Article XIII*

Paragraph 2 (d)

No mention was made of " commercial considerations " as a rule for the allocation of quotas because it was considered that its application by governmental authorities might not always be practicable.   Moreover, in cases where it is practicable, a contracting party could apply these considerations in the process of seeking agreement, consistently with the general rule laid down in the opening sentence of paragraph 2.

Paragraph 4

See note relating to " special factors " in connexion with the last sub-paragraph of paragraph 2 of Article XI.

Ad *Article XIV*

Paragraph 1

The provisions of this paragraph shall not be so construed as to preclude full consideration by the CONTRACTING PARTIES, in the consultations provided for in paragraph 4 of Article XII and in paragraph 12 of Article XVIII, of the nature, effects and reasons for discrimination in the field of import restrictions.

Paragraph 2

One of the situations contemplated in paragraph 2 is that of a contracting party holding balances acquired as a result of current transactions which it finds itself unable to use without a measure of discrimination.

Ad *Article XV*

Paragraph 4

The word " frustrate " is intended to indicate, for example, that infringements of the letter of any Article of this Agreement by exchange action shall not be regarded as a violation of that Article if, in practice, there is no appreciable departure from the intent of the Article.   Thus, a contracting party which, as part of its exchange control operated in accordance with the Articles of Agreement of the International Monetary Fund, requires payment to be received for its exports in its own currency or in the currency of one or more members of the International Monetary Fund will not thereby be deemed to contravene Article XI or Article XIII.   Another example would be that of a contracting party which specifies on an import licence the country from which the goods may be imported, for the purpose not of introducing any additional element of discrimination in its import licensing system but of enforcing permissible exchange controls.

Ad *Article XVI*

The exemption of an exported product from duties or taxes borne by the like product when destined for domestic consumption, or the remission of such duties or taxes in amounts not in excess of those which have accrued, shall not be deemed to be a subsidy.

Section B

1. Nothing in Section B shall preclude the use by a contracting party of multiple rates of exchange in accordance with the Articles of Agreement of the International Monetary Fund.

2. For the purposes of Section B, a " primary product " is understood to be any product of farm, forest or fishery, or any mineral, in its natural form or which has undergone such processing as is customarily required to prepare it for marketing in substantial volume in international trade.

Paragraph 3

1. The fact that a contracting party has not exported the product in question during the previous representative period would not in itself preclude that contracting party from establishing its right to obtain a share of the trade in the product concerned.

2. A system for the stabilization of the domestic price or of the return to domestic producers of a primary product independently of the movements of export prices, which results at times in the sale of the product for export at a price lower than the comparable price charged for the like product to buyers in the domestic market, shall be considered not to involve a subsidy on exports within the meaning of paragraph 3 if the CONTRACTING PARTIES determine that:

(*a*) the system has also resulted, or is so designed as to result, in the sale of the product for export at a price higher than the comparable price charged for the like product to buyers in the domestic market; and

(*b*) the system is so operated, or is designed so to operate, either because of the effective regulation of production or otherwise, as not to stimulate exports unduly or otherwise seriously to prejudice the interests of other contracting parties.

Notwithstanding such determination by the CONTRACTING PARTIES, operations under such a system shall be subject to the provisions of paragraph 3 where they are wholly or partly financed out of government funds in addition to the funds collected from producers in respect of the product concerned.

Paragraph 4

The intention of paragraph 4 is that the contracting parties should seek before the end of 1957 to reach agreement to abolish all remaining subsidies as from 1 January 1958; or, failing this, to reach agreement to extend the application of the standstill until the earliest date thereafter by which they can expect to reach such agreement.

Ad *Article XVII*

Paragraph 1

The operations of Marketing Boards, which are established by contracting parties and are engaged in purchasing or selling, are subject to the provisions of sub-paragraphs (*a*) and (*b*).

The activities of Marketing Boards which are established by contracting parties and which do not purchase or sell but lay down regulations covering private trade are governed by the relevant Articles of this Agreement.

The charging by a state enterprise of different prices for its sales of a product in different markets is not precluded by the provisions of this Article, provided that such different prices are charged for commercial reasons, to meet conditions of supply and demand in export markets.

Paragraph 1 (a)

Governmental measures imposed to ensure standards of quality and efficiency in the operation of external trade, or privileges granted for the exploitation of national natural resources but which do not empower the government to exercise control over the trading activities of the enterprise in question, do not constitute " exclusive or special privileges ".

Paragraph 1 (b)

A country receiving a " tied loan " is free to take this loan into account as a " commercial consideration " when purchasing requirements abroad.

Paragraph 2

The term " goods " is limited to products as understood in commercial practice, and is not intended to include the purchase or sale of services.

Paragraph 3

Negotiations which contracting parties agree to conduct under this paragraph may be directed towards the reduction of duties and other charges on imports and exports or towards the conclusion of any other mutually satisfactory arrangement consistent with the provisions of this Agreement. (See paragraph 4 of Article II and the note to that paragraph.)

Paragraph 4 (b)

The term " import mark-up " in this paragraph shall represent the margin by which the price charged by the import monopoly for the imported product (exclusive of internal taxes within the purview of Article III, transportation, distribution, and other expenses incident to the purchase, sale or further processing, and a reasonable margin of profit) exceeds the landed cost.

Ad *Article XVIII*

The CONTRACTING PARTIES and the contracting parties concerned shall preserve the utmost secrecy in respect of matters arising under this Article.

Paragraphs 1 and 4

1. When they consider whether the economy of a contracting party " can only support low standards of living ", the CONTRACTING PARTIES shall take into consideration the normal position of that economy and shall not base their determination on exceptional circumstances such as those which may result from the temporary existence of exceptionally favourable conditions for the staple export product or products of such contracting party.

2. The phrase " in the early stages of development " is not meant to apply only to contracting parties which have just started their economic development, but also to contracting parties the economies of which are undergoing a process of industrialization to correct an excessive dependence on primary production.

Paragraphs 2, 3, 7, 13 and 22

The reference to the establishment of particular industries shall apply not only to the establishment of a new industry, but also to the establishment of a new branch of production in an existing industry and to the substantial transformation of an existing industry, and to the substantial expansion of an existing industry supplying a relatively small proportion of the domestic demand. It shall also cover the reconstruction of an industry destroyed or substantially damaged as a result of hostilities or natural disasters.

Paragraph 7 (b)

A modification or withdrawal, pursuant to paragraph 7 (*b*), by a contracting party, other than the applicant contracting party, referred to in paragraph 7 (*a*), shall be made within six months of the day on which the action is taken by the applicant contracting party, and shall become effective on the thirtieth day following the day on which such modification or withdrawal has been notified to the CONTRACTING PARTIES.

Paragraph 11

The second sentence in paragraph 11 shall not be interpreted to mean that a contracting party is required to relax or remove restrictions if such relaxation or removal would thereupon produce conditions justifying the intensification or institution, respectively, of restrictions under paragraph 9 of Article XVIII.

Paragraph 12 (b)

The date referred to in paragraph 12 (*b*) shall be the date determined by the CONTRACTING PARTIES in accordance with the provisions of paragraph 4 (*b*) of Article XII of this Agreement.

Paragraphs 13 and 14

It is recognized that, before deciding on the introduction of a measure and notifying the CONTRACTING PARTIES in accordance with paragraph 14, a contracting party may need a reasonable period of time to assess the competitive position of the industry concerned.

Paragraphs 15 and 16

It is understood that the CONTRACTING PARTIES shall invite a contracting party proposing to apply a measure under Section C to consult with them pursuant to paragraph 16 if they are requested to do so by a contracting party the trade of which would be appreciably affected by the measure in question.

Paragraphs 16, 18, 19 and 22

1.   It is understood that the CONTRACTING PARTIES may concur in a proposed measure subject to specific conditions or limitations.   If the measure as applied does not conform to the terms of the concurrence it will to that extent be deemed a measure in which the CONTRACTING PARTIES have not concurred.   In cases in which the CONTRACTING PARTIES have concurred in a measure for a specified period, the contracting party concerned, if it finds that the maintenance of the measure for a further period of time is required to achieve the objective for which the measure was originally taken, may apply to the CONTRACTING PARTIES for an extension of that period in accordance with the provisions and procedures of Section C or D, as the case may be.

2.   It is expected that the CONTRACTING PARTIES will, as a rule, refrain from concurring in a measure which is likely to cause serious prejudice to exports of a commodity on which the economy of a contracting party is largely dependent.

Paragraphs 18 and 22

The phrase " that the interests of other contracting parties are adequately safeguarded " is meant to provide latitude sufficient to permit consideration in each case of the most appropriate method of safeguarding those interests.   The appropriate method may, for instance, take the form of an additional concession to be applied by the contracting party having recourse to Section C or D during such time as the deviation from the other Articles of the Agreement would remain in force or of the temporary suspension by any other contracting party referred to in paragraph 18 of a concession substantially equivalent to the impairment due to the introduction of the measure in question. Such contracting party would have the right to safeguard its interests through such a temporary suspension of a concession; *Provided* that this right will not be exercised when, in the case of a measure imposed by a contracting party coming within the scope of paragraph 4 (*a*), the CONTRACTING PARTIES have determined that the extent of the compensatory concession proposed was adequate.

Paragraph 19

The provisions of paragraph 19 are intended to cover the cases where an industry has been in existence beyond the " reasonable period of time " referred to in the note to paragraphs 13 and 14, and should not be so construed as to deprive a contracting party coming within the scope of paragraph 4 (*a*) of Article XVIII, of its right to resort to the other provisions of Section C, including paragraph 17, with regard to a newly established industry even though it has benefited from incidental protection afforded by balance of payments import restrictions.

Paragraph 21

Any measure taken pursuant to the provisions of paragraph 21 shall be withdrawn forthwith if the action taken in accordance with paragraph 17 is withdrawn or if the CONTRACTING PARTIES concur in the measure proposed after the expiration of the ninety-day time limit specified in paragraph 17.

Ad *Article XX*
Sub-paragraph (h)

The exception provided for in this sub-paragraph extends to any commodity agreement which conforms to the principles approved by the Economic and Social Council in its resolution 30 (IV) of 28 March 1947.

Ad *Article XXIV*
Paragraph 9

It is understood that the provisions of Article I would require that, when a product which has been imported into the territory of a member of a customs union or free-trade area at a preferential rate of duty is re-exported to the territory of another member of such union or area, the latter member should collect a duty equal to the difference between the duty already paid and any higher duty that would be payable if the product were being imported directly into its territory.

Paragraph 11

Measures adopted by India and Pakistan in order to carry out definitive trade arrangements between them, once they have been agreed upon, might depart from particular provisions of this Agreement, but these measures would in general be consistent with the objectives of the Agreement.

Ad *Article XXVIII*

The CONTRACTING PARTIES and each contracting party concerned should arrange to conduct the negotiations and consultations with the greatest possible secrecy in order to avoid premature disclosure of details of prospective tariff changes. The CONTRACTING PARTIES shall be informed immediately of all changes in national tariffs resulting from recourse to this Article.

Paragraph 1

1. If the CONTRACTING PARTIES specify a period other than a three-year period, a contracting party may act pursuant to paragraph 1 or paragraph 3 of Article XXVIII on the first day following the expiration of such other period and, unless the CONTRACTING PARTIES have again specified another period, subsequent periods will be three-year periods following the expiration of such specified period.

2. The provision that on 1 January 1958, and on other days determined pursuant to paragraph 1, a contracting party "may ... modify or withdraw a concession" means that on such day, and on the first day after the end of each period, the legal obligation of such contracting party under Article II is altered; it does not mean that the changes in its customs tariff should necessarily be made effective on that day. If a tariff change resulting from negotiations undertaken pursuant to this Article is delayed, the entry into force of any compensatory concessions may be similarly delayed.

3. Not earlier than six months, nor later than three months, prior to 1 January 1958, or to the termination date of any subsequent period, a contracting party wishing to modify or withdraw any concession embodied in the appropriate Schedule, should notify the CONTRACTING PARTIES to this effect. The CONTRACTING PARTIES shall then determine the contracting party or contracting parties with which the negotiations or consultations referred to in paragraph 1 shall take place. Any contracting party so determined shall participate in such negotiations or consultations with the applicant contracting party with the aim of reaching agreement before the end of the period. Any extension of the assured life of the Schedules shall relate to the Schedules as modified after such negotiations, in accordance with paragraphs 1, 2 and 3 of Article XXVIII. If the CONTRACTING PARTIES are arranging for multilateral tariff negotiations to take place within the period of six months before 1 January 1958, or before any other day determined pursuant to paragraph 1, they shall include in the arrangements for such negotiations suitable procedures for carrying out the negotiations referred to in this paragraph.

4. The object of providing for the participation in the negotiations of any contracting party with a principal supplying interest, in addition to any contracting party with which the concession was initially negotiated, is to ensure that a contracting party with a larger share in the trade affected by the concession than a contracting party with which the concession was initially negotiated shall have an effective opportunity to protect the contractual right which it enjoys under this

171

Agreement. On the other hand, it is not intended that the scope of the negotiations should be such as to make negotiations and agreement under Article XXVIII unduly difficult nor to create complications in the application of this Article in the future to concessions which result from negotiations thereunder. Accordingly, the CONTRACTING PARTIES should only determine that a contracting party has a principal supplying interest if that contracting party has had, over a reasonable period of time prior to the negotiations, a larger share in the market of the applicant contracting party than a contracting party with which the concession was initially negotiated or would, in the judgment of the CONTRACTING PARTIES, have had such a share in the absence of discriminatory quantitative restrictions maintained by the applicant contracting party. It would therefore not be appropriate for the CONTRACTING PARTIES to determine that more than one contracting party, or in those exceptional cases where there is near equality more than two contracting parties, had a principal supplying interest.

5. Notwithstanding the definition of a principal supplying interest in note 4 to paragraph 1, the CONTRACTING PARTIES may exceptionally determine that a contracting party has a principal supplying interest if the concession in question affects trade which constitutes a major part of the total exports of such contracting party.

6. It is not intended that provision for participation in the negotiations of any contracting party with a principal supplying interest, and for consultation with any contracting party having a substantial interest in the concession which the applicant contracting party is seeking to modify or withdraw, should have the effect that it should have to pay compensation or suffer retaliation greater than the withdrawal or modification sought, judged in the light of the conditions of trade at the time of the proposed withdrawal or modification, making allowance for any discriminatory quantitative restrictions maintained by the applicant contracting party.

7. The expression " substantial interest " is not capable of a precise definition and accordingly may present difficulties for the CONTRACTING PARTIES. It is, however, intended to be construed to cover only those contracting parties which have, or in the absence of discriminatory quantitative restrictions affecting their exports could reasonably be expected to have, a significant share in the market of the contracting party seeking to modify or withdraw the concession.

Paragraph 4

1. Any request for authorization to enter into negotiations shall be accompanied by all relevant statistical and other data. A decision on such request shall be made within thirty days of its submission.

2. It is recognized that to permit certain contracting parties, depending in large measure on a relatively small number of primary commodities and relying on the tariff as an important aid for furthering diversification of their economies or as an important source of revenue, normally to negotiate for the modification or withdrawal of concessions only under paragraph 1 of Article XXVIII, might cause them at such a time to make modifications or withdrawals which in the long

run would prove unnecessary. To avoid such a situation the CONTRACTING PARTIES shall authorize any such contracting party, under paragraph 4, to enter into negotiations unless they consider this would result in, or contribute substantially towards, such an increase in tariff levels as to threaten the stability of the Schedules to this Agreement or lead to undue disturbance of international trade.

3. It is expected that negotiations authorized under paragraph 4 for modification or withdrawal of a single item, or a very small group of items, could normally be brought to a conclusion in sixty days. It is recognized, however, that such a period will be inadequate for cases involving negotiations for the modification or withdrawal of a larger number of items and in such cases, therefore, it would be appropriate for the CONTRACTING PARTIES to prescribe a longer period.

4. The determination referred to in paragraph 4 (*d*) shall be made by the CONTRACTING PARTIES within thirty days of the submission of the matter to them unless the applicant contracting party agrees to a longer period.

5. In determining under paragraph 4 (*d*) whether an applicant contracting party has unreasonably failed to offer adequate compensation, it is understood that the CONTRACTING PARTIES will take due account of the special position of a contracting party which has bound a high proportion of its tariffs at very low rates of duty and to this extent has less scope than other contracting parties to make compensatory adjustment.

Ad *Article XXVIII* bis

Paragraph 3

It is understood that the reference to fiscal needs would include the revenus aspect of duties and particularly duties imposed primarily for revenue purpose, or duties imposed on products which can be substituted for products subject to revenue duties to prevent the avoidance of such duties.

Ad *Article XXIX*

Paragraph 1

Chapters VII and VIII of the Havana Charter have been excluded from paragraph 1 because they generally deal with the organization, functions and procedures of the International Trade Organization.

Ad *Part IV*

The words " developed contracting parties " and the words " less-developed contracting parties " as used in Part IV are to be understood to refer to developed and less-developed countries which are parties to the General Agreement on Tariffs and Trade.

Ad *Article XXXVI*

Paragraph 1

This Article is based upon the objectives set forth in Article I as it will be amended by Section A of paragraph 1 of the Protocol Amending Part I and Articles XXIX and XXX when that Protocol enters into force. [1]

Paragraph 4

The term " primary products " includes agricultural products, *vide* paragraph 2 of the note ad Article XVI, Section B.

Paragraph 5

A diversification programme would generally include the intensification of activities for the processing of primary products and the development of manufacturing industries, taking into account the situation of the particular contracting party and the world outlook for production and consumption of different commodities.

Paragraph 8

It is understood that the phrase " do not expect reciprocity " means, in accordance with the objectives set forth in this Article, that the less-developed contracting parties should not be expected, in the course of trade negotiations, to make contributions which are inconsistent with their individual development, financial and trade needs, taking into consideration past trade developments.

This paragraph would apply in the event of action under Section A of Article XVIII, Article XXVIII, Article XXVIII *bis* (Article XXIX after the amendment set forth in Section A of paragraph 1 of the Protocol Amending Part I and Articles XXIX and XXX shall have become effective [1]), Article XXXIII, or any other procedure under this Agreement.

Ad *Article XXXVII*

Paragraph 1 (a)

This paragraph would apply in the event of negotiations for reduction or elimination of tariffs or other restrictive regulations of commerce under Articles XXVIII, XXVIII *bis* (XXIX after the amendment set forth in Section A of paragraph 1 of the Protocol Amending Part I and Articles XXIX and XXX shall have become effective [1]), and Article XXXIII, as well as in connexion with other action to effect such reduction or elimination which contracting parties may be able to undertake.

Paragraph 3 (b)

The other measures referred to in this paragraph might include steps to promote domestic structural changes, to encourage the consumption of particular products, or to introduce measures of trade promotion.

---

[1] This Protocol was abandoned on 1 January 1968.

PROTOCOL OF PROVISIONAL APPLICATION
OF THE GENERAL AGREEMENT ON TARIFFS AND TRADE

1. The Governments of the COMMONWEALTH OF AUSTRALIA, the KINGDOM OF BELGIUM (in respect of its metropolitan territory), CANADA, the FRENCH REPUBLIC (in respect of its metropolitan territory), the GRAND-DUCHY OF LUXEMBURG, the KINGDOM OF THE NETHERLANDS (in respect of its metropolitan territory), the UNITED KINGDOM OF GREAT BRITAIN AND NORTHERN IRELAND (in respect of its metropolitan territory), and the UNITED STATES OF AMERICA, undertake, provided that this Protocol shall have been signed on behalf of all the foregoing Governments not later than 15 November 1947, to apply provisionally on and after 1 January 1948:

    (*a*) Parts I and III of the General Agreement on Tariffs and Trade, and

    (*b*) Part II of that Agreement to the fullest extent not inconsistent with existing legislation.

2. The foregoing Governments shall make effective such provisional application of the General Agreement, in respect of any of their territories other than their metropolitan territories, on or after 1 January 1948, upon the expiration of thirty days from the day on which notice of such application is received by the Secretary-General of the United Nations.

3. Any other government signatory to this Protocol shall make effective such provisional application of the General Agreement, on or after 1 January 1948, upon the expiration of thirty days from the day of signature of this Protocol on behalf of such Government.

4. This Protocol shall remain open for signature at the Headquarters of the United Nations (*a*) until 15 November 1947, on behalf of any government named in paragraph 1 of this Protocol which has not signed it on this day, and (*b*) until 30 June 1948, on behalf of any other Government signatory to the Final Act adopted at the conclusion of the Second Session of the Preparatory Committee of the United Nations Conference on Trade and Employment which has not signed it on this day.

5. Any government applying this Protocol shall be free to withdraw such application, and such withdrawal shall take effect upon the expiration of sixty days from the day on which written notice of such withdrawal is received by the Secretary-General of the United Nations.

6.   The original of this Protocol shall be deposited with the Secretary-General of the United Nations, who will furnish certified copies thereof to all interested Governments.

IN WITNESS WHEREOF the respective Representatives, after having communicated their full powers, found to be in good and due form, have signed the Protocol.

DONE at Geneva, in a single copy, in the English and French languages, both texts authentic, this thirtieth day of October one thousand nine hundred and forty-seven.

APPENDIX

The first section of this Appendix gives the source (legal instruments) of the various provisions of the GATT, other than schedules, their effective date and their respective citations in the United Nations *Treaty Series* (UNTS) or in GATT publications.

The second section contains a key to the abbreviated titles used in the first section, together with their citations.   Column 4 refers to provisions in Part I of the General Agreement and indicates where they have been qualified, for instance, with regard to territorial application or the maintenance of preferences.   Column 5 refers to provisions in Part II of the General Agreement, and indicates where they have been qualified, e.g. with regard to dates of application.   Column 6 refers to different applicable dates with regard to paragraph 1 of Article II.   Column 7 refers to different applicable dates with regard to Article V: 6, Article VII: 4 (*d*), Article X: 3 (*c*).   Column 8 refers to different termination periods for withdrawal from the Agreement.

I. SOURCE AND EFFECTIVE DATE OF GATT PROVISIONS

GATT provision	Source	Effective	Citation
Title	GATT	1 Jan. 1948	55 UNTS 194
Preamble	GATT	1 Jan. 1948	55 UNTS 194
Part I	GATT	1 Jan. 1948	55 UNTS 196
Article 1	GATT	1 Jan. 1948	55 UNTS 196
Par. 1	Cross reference to art. III modified by 1948 Pt. I Prot., par. 1, sec. A (i)	24 Sept. 1952	138 UNTS 336
Par. 2	Cross reference to subsequent par. modified by 1948 Pt. I Prot., par. 1, sec. A (ii)	24 Sept. 1952	138 UNTS 336
	Provisions in supplementary agreements permitting additional tariff preferences are listed in col. 4 of key in section II		
Par. 3	1948 Pt. I Prot., par. 1, sec. A (iii)	24 Sept. 1952	138 UNTS 336
Par. 4	Par. No. modified by 1948 Pt. I Prot., par. 1, sec. A (iii)	24 Sept. 1952	138 UNTS 336
	Provisions in supplementary agreements providing different base dates are listed in col. 4 of key in section II		
Article II	GATT	1 Jan. 1948	55 UNTS 200
Par. 1	Provisions in supplementary agreements providing different dates applicable to certain concessions are listed in col. 6 of key in section II		
Par. 2 Subpar. (a)	Cross reference to art. III modified by 1948 Pt. I Prot., par. 1, sec. B	24 Sept. 1952	138 UNTS 336

GATT provision	Source	Effective	Citation
Part I (cont.)			
Article II (cont.)			
Par. 6			
Subpar. (a)	Provisions in supplementary agreements providing different dates applicable to certain concessions are listed in col. 6 of key in section II		
Part II	GATT	1 Jan. 1948	55 UNTS 204
	Provisions in supplementary agreements qualifying application of this part are listed in col. 5 of key in section II		
Article III	1948 Pt. II Prot., par. 1, sec. A	14 Dec. 1948	62 UNTS 82
Article IV	GATT	1 Jan. 1948	55 UNTS 208
Article V	GATT	1 Jan. 1948	55 UNTS 208
Par. 6	Provisions in supplementary agreements providing different dates concerning consignment requirements are listed in col. 7 of key in section II		
Article VI	1948 Pt. II Prot., par. 1, sec. B	14 Dec. 1948	62 UNTS 86
Par. 6	1955 Pt. II Prot., par. 1, sec. D	7 Oct. 1957	278 UNTS 170
Article VII	GATT	1 Jan. 1948	55 UNTS 216
Par. 1	Former qualification deleted from first sentence by 1955 Pt. II Prot., par. 1, sec. E (i)	7 Oct. 1957	278 UNTS 172
Par. 2			
Subpar. (b)	First sentence modified by 1955 Pt. II Prot., par. 1, sec. E (ii)	7 Oct. 1957	278 UNTS 172
Par. 4			
Subpar. (a) and (b)	Modified by 1955 Pt. II Prot., par. 1, sec. E (iii)	7 Oct. 1957	278 UNTS 172
Subpar. (d)	Provisions in supplementary agreements providing different dates concerning currency conversion methods are listed in col. 7 of key in section II		

GATT provision	Source	Effective	Citation
Part II (*cont.*)			
Article VIII	GATT	1 Jan. 1948	55 UNTS 218
Title	1955 Pt. II Prot., par. 1, sec. F (i)	7 Oct. 1957	278 UNTS 174
Par. 1 and 2	1955 Pt. II Prot., par. 1, sec. F (ii)	7 Oct. 1957	278 UNTS 174
Article IX	GATT	1 Jan. 1948	55 UNTS 220
Par. 2	1955 Pt. II Prot., par. 1, sec. G (i)	7 Oct. 1957	278 UNTS 174
Par. 3 to 6	Par. No. modified by 1955 Pt. II Prot., par. 1, sec. G (ii)	7 Oct. 1957	278 UNTS 174
Article X	GATT	1 Jan. 1948	55 UNTS 222
Par. 3 Subpar. (*c*)	Provisions in supplementary agreements providing different dates concerning procedures are listed in col. 7 of key in section II		
Article XI	GATT	1 Jan. 1948	55 UNTS 224
	Former par. 3 deleted by 1955 Pt. II Prot., par. 1, sec. H	7 Oct. 1957	278 UNTS 174
Article XII	1955 Pt. II Prot., par. 1, sec. I	7 Oct. 1957	278 UNTS 174
Article XIII	GATT	1 Jan. 1948	55 UNTS 234
Par. 5	Former reference to art. III deleted by 1948 Pt. II Prot., par. 1, sec. C	14 Dec. 1948	62 UNTS 90
Article XIV			
Par. 1	1955 Pt. II Prot., par. 1, sec. J (i)	15 Feb. 1961	278 UNTS 180
Par. 2 to 5	1955 Pt. II Prot., par. 1, sec. J (ii)	7 Oct. 1957	278 UNTS 180
Article XV	GATT	1 Jan. 1948	55 UNTS 246
Par. 2	Reference to art. XVIII added by 1955 Pt. II Prot., par. 1, sec. K	7 Oct. 1957	278 UNTS 182
Par. 9	Opening clause modified by 1948 Pt. II, Prot., par. 1, sec. D	14 Dec. 1948	62 UNTS 90

GATT provision	Source	Effective	Citation
Part II (*cont.*)			
Article XVI	GATT	1 Jan. 1948	55 UNTS 250
Sec. A			
Title	Section designation and title added by 1955 Pt. II Prot., par. 1, sec. L (i)	7 Oct. 1957	278 UNTS 182
Par. 1	Par. No. added by 1955 Pt. II Prot., par. 1, sec. L (i)	7 Oct. 1957	278 UNTS 182
Sec. B	1955 Pt. II Prot., par. 1, sec. L (ii)	7 Oct. 1957	278 UNTS 182
Par. 2	Opening words modified by 1955 Rectif. P.-V., art. I, sec. B, par. 4	7 Oct. 1957	278 UNTS 248
Par. 4	Effective date of prohibition provided for in 1960 art. XVI:4 Prohib. Decl., par. 1	14 Nov. 1962	445 UNTS 294
	Reference to domestic market modified by 1955 Rectif. P.-V., art. I, sec. B, par. 4	7 Oct. 1957	278 UNTS 248
Article XVII	GATT	1 Jan. 1948	55 UNTS 250
Title	Modified by 1955 Pt. II Prot., par. 1, sec. M (i)	7 Oct. 1957	278 UNTS 184
Par. 3 and 4	1955 Pt. II Prot., par. 1, sec. M (ii)	7 Oct. 1957	278 UNTS 184
Article XVIII	1955 Pt. II Prot., par. 1, sec. N	7 Oct. 1957	278 UNTS 186
Article XIX	GATT	1 Jan. 1948	55 UNTS 258
Par. 3	Language of suspension rights modified by 1955 Pt. II Prot., par. 1, sec. O	7 Oct. 1957	278 UNTS 200
Article XX	GATT	1 Jan. 1948	55 UNTS 262
	Former Pt. II and No. of Pt. I deleted by 1955 Pt. II Prot., par. 1, sec. P (i)	7 Oct. 1957	278 UNTS 200
Subpar. (*h*)	1955 Pt. II Prot., par. 1, sec. P (ii)	7 Oct. 1957	278 UNTS 200
Subpar. (*j*)	1955 Pt. II Prot., par. 1, sec. P (iii)	7 Oct. 1957	278 UNTS 200
Article XXI	GATT	1 Jan. 1948	55 UNTS 266
Article XXII	1955 Pt. II Prot., par. 1, sec. Q	7 Oct. 1957	278 UNTS 200
Article XXIII	GATT	1 Jan. 1948	55 UNTS 266
Par. 2	Last two sentences modified by 1955 Pt. II Prot., par. 1, sec. R	7 Oct. 1957	278 UNTS 200

GATT provision	Source	Effective	Citation
Part III	GATT	1 Jan. 1948	55 UNTS 268
Article XXIV	1948 art. XXIV Prot., sec. I	7 June 1948	62 UNTS 56
Par. 4	1955 Pt. II Prot., par. 1, sec. S (i)	7 Oct. 1957	278 UNTS 202
Par. 7			
Subpar. (*b*)	First clause modified by 1955 Pt. II Prot., par. 1, sec. S (ii)	7 Oct. 1957	278 UNTS 202
Article XXV	GATT	1 Jan. 1948	55 UNTS 272
Par. 5	1948 Mod. Prot., sec. 1	15 Apr. 1948	62 UNTS 30
	Former subpars. (*b*) through (*d*) and subpar. designation following par. no. deleted by 1955 Pt. II Prot., par. 1, sec. T	7 Oct. 1957	278 UNTS 202
Article XXVI	1955 Pt. II Prot., par. 1, sec. U (i)	7 Oct. 1957	278 UNTS 202
Article XXVII	GATT	1 Jan. 1948	55 UNTS 276
	Final sentence modified by 1955 Pt. II Prot., par. 1, sec. V	7 Oct. 1957	278 UNTS 204
Article XXVIII	1955 Pt. II Prot., par. 1, sec. W	7 Oct. 1957	278 UNTS 204
Article XXVIII *bis*	1955 Pt. II Prot., par. 1, sec. X (i)	7 Oct. 1957	278 UNTS 208
Article XXIX	1948 Pt. I Prot., par. 1, sec. C	24 Sept. 1952	138 UNTS 336
Article XXX	GATT	1 Jan. 1948	55 UNTS 282
Article XXXI	GATT	1 Jan. 1948	55 UNTS 282
	Reference to art. XVIII added by 1955 Pt. II Prot., par. 1, sec. Y (i)	7 Oct. 1957	278 UNTS 210
	Connecting words added to first clause by 1955 Rectif. P.-V., art. I, sec. B, par. 5	7 Oct. 1957	278 UNTS 248
	Former limiting date deleted from each sentence by 1955 Pt. II Prot., par. 1, sec. Y (ii) and (iii)	7 Oct. 1957	278 UNTS 210
	Provisions in supplementary agreements providing for different termination period are listed in col. 8 of key in section II		

GATT provision	Source	Effective	Citation
Part III (*cont.*)			
Article XXXII	GATT	1 Jan. 1948	55 UNTS 282
Par. 1	1948 Mod. Prot., sec. II	15 Apr. 1948	62 UNTS 32
Par. 2	Cross references modified by 1955 Pt. II Prot., par. 1, sec. SS	7 Oct. 1957	278 UNTS 234
Article XXXIII	1948 Mod. Prot., sec. III	15 Apr. 1948	62 UNTS 34
Article XXXIV	GATT	1 Jan. 1948	55 UNTS 284
Article XXXV	1955 Pt. II Prot., par. 1, sec. Z	7 Oct. 1957	278 UNTS 210
Part IV	1965 Pt. IV Prot., par. 1, sec. A	27 June 1966	GATT, Final Act 2nd Sp. Sess. 25
Article XXXVI	1965 Pt. IV Prot., par. 1, sec. A	27 June 1966	GATT, Final Act 2nd Sp. Sess. 25
Article XXXVII	1965 Pt. IV Prot., par. 1, sec. A	27 June 1966	GATT, Final Act 2nd Sp. Sess. 27
Article XXXVIII	1965 Pt. IV Prot., par. 1, sec. A	27 June 1966	GATT, Final Act 2nd Sp. Sess. 30
Annex A	GATT	1 Jan. 1948	55 UNTS 284
Final par.	1948 Pt. I Prot., par. 1, sec. D	24 Sept. 1952	138 UNTS 338
Annex B	1955 4th Rectif. and Modif. Prot., par. 1	23 Jan. 1959	324 UNTS 302
Annex C	1950 4th Rectif. Prot., par. 1 (*a*)	24 Sept. 1952	138 UNTS 399
	Last name in list modified by 1950 5th Rectif. Prot., par. 1 (*a*)	30 June 1953	167 UNTS 266
Annex D	GATT	1 Jan. 1948	55 UNTS 290
Annex E	GATT	1 Jan. 1948	55 UNTS 290
Annex F	GATT	1 Jan. 1948	55 UNTS 290
Annex G	GATT	1 Jan. 1948	55 UNTS 290
Annex H	1955 Pt. II Prot., par. 1, sec. AA (i)	7 Oct. 1957	278 UNTS 212
Annex I	GATT	1 Jan. 1948	55 UNTS 292
Title	1955 Pt. II Prot., par. 1, sec. BB (ii)	7 Oct. 1957	278 UNTS 214

GATT provision	Source	Effective	Citation
Annex I (*cont.*)			
Ad Article I	GATT	1 Jan. 1948	55 UNTS 292
Par. 1			
First par.	Cross reference to art. III modified by 1948 Pt. I Prot., par. 1, sec. E (i)	24 Sept. 1948	138 UNTS 338
Second par.	1948 Pt. I Prot., par. 1, sec. E (ii)	24 Sept. 1952	138 UNTS 338
Par. 3	Par. No. modified by 1948 Pt. I Prot., par. 1, sec. E (iii)	24 Sept. 1952	138 UNTS 340
Ad Article II	GATT	1 Jan. 1948	55 UNTS 294
Par. 2 (*a*)	1948 Pt. I Prot., par. 1, sec. E (iv)	24 Sept. 1952	138 UNTS 340
Par. 4	1948 Pt. I Prot., par. 1, sec. E (v)	24 Sept. 1952	138 UNTS 340
Ad Article III	1948 Pt. II Prot., par. 1, sec. G (i)	14 Dec. 1948	62 UNTS 104
Ad Article V	GATT	1 Jan. 1948	55 UNTS 296
Ad Article VI	1948 Pt. II Prot., par. 1, sec. G (ii)	14 Dec. 1948	62 UNTS 106
Par. 1			
Note 1	Note No. added by 1955 Pt. II Prot., par. 1, sec. CC (i)	7 Oct. 1957	278 UNTS 214
Note 2	1955 Pt. II Prot., par. 1, sec. CC (ii)	7 Oct. 1957	278 UNTS 214
Par. 6 (*b*)	1955 Pt. II Prot., par. 1, sec. CC (iii)	7 Oct. 1957	278 UNTS 214
Ad Article VII	GATT	1 Jan. 1948	55 UNTS 296
Par. 1	1955 Pt. II Prot., par. 1, sec. DD (i)	7 Oct. 1957	278 UNTS 214
Par. 2	1955 Pt. II Prot., par. 1, sec. DD (ii)	7 Oct. 1957	278 UNTS 214
Ad Article VIII	1955 Pt. II Prot., par. 1, sec. EE	7 Oct. 1957	278 UNTS 216
Ad Articles XI, XII, XIII, XIV and XVIII	1955 Rectif. P.-V., art. I, sec. B, par. 7	7 Oct. 1957	278 UNTS 248
Ad Article XI	GATT	1 Jan. 1948	55 UNTS 298
Ad Article XII	1955 Pt. II Prot., par. 1, sec. GG	7 Oct. 1957	278 UNTS 216

GATT provision	Source	Effective	Citation
Annex I (*cont.*)			
Ad Article XIII	GATT	1 Jan. 1948	55 UNTS 300
Ad Article XIV			
Par. 1	1955 Pt. II Prot., par. 1, sec. HH	15 Feb. 1961	278 UNTS 218
Par. 2	1948 Art. XIV Prot., sec. II	1 Jan. 1949	62 UNTS 46
Ad Article XV	GATT	1 Jan. 1948	55 UNTS 302
Ad Article XVI	1955 Pt. II Prot., par. 1, sec. II	7 Oct. 1957	278 UNTS 218
Ad Article XVII	GATT	1 Jan. 1948	55 UNTS 302
Par. 3	1955 Pt. II Prot., par. 1, sec. JJ	7 Oct. 1957	278 UNTS 220
Par. 4 (*b*)	1955 Pt. II Prot., par. 1, sec. JJ	7 Oct. 1957	278 UNTS 220
Ad Article XVIII	1955 Pt. II Prot., par. 1, sec. KK	7 Oct. 1957	278 UNTS 222
Ad Article XX	1955 Pt. II Prot., par. 1, sec. LL	7 Oct. 1957	278 UNTS 226
Ad Article XXIV	1948 Art. XXIV Prot., sec. II	7 June 1948	62 UNTS 64
Par. 9	1949 3rd Rectif. Prot., par. 1	21 Oct. 1951	107 UNTS 314
Ad Article XXVIII	1955 Pt. II Prot., par. 1, sec. NN	7 Oct. 1957	278 UNTS 226
Ad Article XXVIII *bis*	1955 Pt. II Prot., par. 1, sec. OO (i)	7 Oct. 1957	278 UNTS 232
Ad Article XXIX	1948 Pt. I Prot., par. 1, sec. E (vi)	24 Sept. 1952	138 UNTS 340
Ad Part IV	1965 Pt. IV Prot., par. 1, sec. B	27 June 1966	GATT, Final Act 2nd Sp. Sess. 31
Ad Article XXXVI	1965 Pt. IV Prot., par. 1, sec. B	27 June 1966	GATT, Final Act 2nd Sp. Sess. 31
Ad Article XXXVII	1965 Pt. IV Prot., par. 1, sec. B	27 June 1966	GATT, Final Act 2nd Sp. Sess. 32

II. KEY TO ABBREVIATIONS USED IN THIS APPENDIX AND TO PROVISIONS IN SUPPLEMENTARY AGREEMENTS AFFECTING THE APPLICATION OF CERTAIN PORTIONS OF THE GENERAL AGREEMENT

Abbreviated agreement title used (1)	Agreement title (2)	Citation (3)	Qualification re application of pt. I (4)	Qualification re application of pt. II (5)	Different date re certain concessions (6)	Different date re certain parties (7)	Different termination period (8)
GATT	General Agreement on Tariffs and Trade	55 UNTS 194	—	—	—	—	—
—	Protocol of Provisional Application of the General Agreement on Tariffs and Trade, 30 October 1947	55 UNTS 308	—	Par. 1 (*b*)	—	—	Par. 5
1948 Mod. Prot.	Protocol modifying certain provisions of the General Agreement on Tariffs and Trade, 24 March 1948	62 UNTS 30	—	—	—	—	—
1948 Art. XIV Prot.	Special Protocol modifying Article XIV of the General Agreement on Tariffs and Trade, 24 March 1948	62 UNTS 40	—	—	—	—	—
1948 Art. XXIV Prot.	Special Protocol relating to Article XXIV of the General Agreement on Tariffs and Trade, 24 March 1948	62 UNTS 56	—	—	—	—	—
1948 Pt. I Prot.	Protocol modifying Part I and Article XXIX of the General Agreement on Tariffs and Trade, 14 September 1948	138 UNTS 334	—	—	—	—	—

1948 Pt. II Prot.	Protocol modifying Part II and Article XXVI of the General Agreement on Tariffs and Trade, 14 September 1948	62 UNTS 80	—	—	—	—	—
—	Protocol for the Accession of Signatories of the Final Act of 30 October 1947, 14 September 1948	62 UNTS 68	—	Par. 1	—	—	Par. 1
1949 3rd Rectif. Prot.	Third Protocol of Rectifications to the General Agreement on Tariffs and Trade, 13 August 1949	107 UNTS 312	—	—	—	—	—
—	Annecy Protocol of Terms of Accession to the General Agreement on Tariffs and Trade, 10 October 1949	62 UNTS 122	Par. 1 (d)	Par. 1 (a) (ii)	Par. 5 (a)	Par. 5 (b)	Par. 7
1950 4th Rectif. Prot.	Fourth Protocol of Rectifications to the General Agreement on Tariffs and Trade, 3 April 1950	138 UNTS 398	—	—	—	—	—
1950 5th Rectif. Prot.	Fifth Protocol of Rectifications to the General Agreement on Tariffs and Trade, 16 December 1950	167 UNTS 265	—	—	—	—	—
—	Torquay Protocol to the General Agreement on Tariffs and Trade, 21 April 1951	142 UNTS 34	—	Par. 1 (a) (ii)	Par. 5 (a)	Par. 5 (b)	Par. 8
—	First Protocol of Supplementary Concessions to the General Agreement on Tariffs and Trade (Union of South Africa and Germany), 27 October 1951	131 UNTS 316	—	—	Par. 3	—	—

Abbreviated agreement title used (1)	Agreement title (2)	Citation (3)	Qualification re application of pt. I (4)	Qualification re application of pt. II (5)	Different date re certain concessions (6)	Different date re certain parties (7)	Different termination period (8)
—	Second Protocol of Supplementary Concessions to the General Agreement on Tariffs and Trade (Austria and Germany), 22 November 1952	172 UNTS 340	—	—	Par. 3	—	—
1955 4th Rectif. & Modif. Prot.	Fourth Protocol of Rectifications and Modifications to the Annexes and to the Texts of the Schedules to the General Agreement on Tariffs and Trade, 7 March 1955	324 UNTS 300	—	—	—	—	—
1955 Pt. II Prot.	Protocol Amending the Preamble and Parts II and III of the General Agreement on Tariffs and Trade, 10 March 1955	278 UNTS 168	—	—	—	—	—
—	Protocol of Terms of Accession of Japan to the General Agreement on Tariffs and Trade, 7 June 1955	220 UNTS 164	Par. 1 (d)	Par. 1 (a) (ii)	Par. 5 (a)	Par. 5 (b)	Par. 7
—	Third Protocol of Supplementary Concessions to the General Agreement on Tariffs and Trade (Denmark and Federal Republic of Germany), 15 July 1955	250 UNTS 292	—	—	Par. 2 (a)	—	—

—	Fourth Protocol of Supplementary Concessions to the General Agreement on Tariffs and Trade (Federal Republic of Germany and Norway), 15 July 1955	250 UNTS 297	—	—	—	Par. 2 (*a*)	—	—
—	Fifth Protocol of Supplementary Concessions to the General Agreement on Tariffs and Trade (Federal Republic of Germany and Sweden), 15 July 1955	250 UNTS 301	—	—	—	Par. 2 (*a*)	—	—
1955 Rectif. P.-V.	Procès-Verbal of Rectification Concerning the Protocol Amending Part I and Articles XXIX and XXX of the General Agreement on Tariffs and Trade, the Protocol amending the Preamble and Parts II and III of the General Agreement on Tariffs and Trade and the Protocol of Organizational Amendments to the General Agreement on Tariffs and Trade, 3 December 1955	278 UNTS 246	—	—	—	—	—	—
—	Sixth Protocol of Supplementary Concessions to the General Agreement on Tariffs and Trade, 23 May 1956	244 UNTS 2	—	—	—	Par. 4	—	—
—	Seventh Protocol of Supplementary Concessions to the General Agreement on Tariffs and Trade (Austria and Federal Republic of Germany), 19 February 1957	309 UNTS 364	—	—	—	Par. 4	—	—

Abbreviated agreement title used (1)	Agreement title (2)	Citation (3)	Qualification re application of pt. I (4)	Qualification re application of pt. II (5)	Different date re certain concessions (6)	Different date re certain parties (7)	Different termination period (8)
—	Eighth Protocol of Supplementary Concessions to the General Agreement on Tariffs and Trade (Cuba and United States of America), 20 June 1957	274 UNTS 322	—	—	Par. 2	—	—
—	Protocol relating to Negotiations for the Establishment of New Schedule III—Brazil—to the General Agreement on Tariffs and Trade, 31 December 1958	398 UNTS 318	—	—	Par. 7	—	—
1960 Art. XVI: 4 Prohib. Decl.	Declaration Giving Effect to the Provisions of Article XVI: 4 of the General Agreement on Tariffs and Trade, 19 November 1960	445 UNTS 294	—	—	—	—	—
—	Protocol for the Accession of Portugal to the General Agreement on Tariffs and Trade, 6 April 1962	431 UNTS 208	Par. 3	Par. 1 (b)	Par. 7	Par. 2 (b)	Par. 12
—	Protocol for the Accession of Israel to the General Agreement on Tariffs and Trade, 6 April 1962	431 UNTS 244	—	Par. 1 (b)	Par. 6	Par. 2 (b)	Par. 10

—	Protocol to the General Agreement on Tariffs and Trade Embodying Results of the 1960-61 Tariff Conference, 16 July 1962	440 UNTS 2	—	—	Par. 5	—	—
—	Tenth Protocol of Supplementary Concessions to the General Agreement on Tariffs and Trade (Japan and New Zealand), 28 January 1963	476 UNTS 254	—	—	Par. 4	—	—
—	Protocol Supplementary to the Protocol to the General Agreement on Tariffs and Trade Embodying Results of the 1960-61 Tariff Conference, 6 May 1963	501 UNTS 304	—	—	Par. 4	—	—
—	Protocol for the Accession of Spain to the General Agreement on Tariffs and Trade, 1 July 1963	476 UNTS 264	Par. 4	Par. 1 (b)	Par. 8	Par. 2 (b)	Par. 12
1965 Pt. IV Prot.	Protocol Amending the General Agreement on Tariffs and Trade to Introduce a Part IV on Trade and Development, 8 February 1965	GATT, Final Act 2nd Sp. Sess. 25	—	—	—	—	—
—	Protocol for the Accession of Switzerland to the General Agreement on Tariffs and Trade, 1 April 1966	GATT, Prot. Acc. Switz.	—	Pars. 1 (b), 4, and 5	Par. 9	Par. 2 (b)	Par. 15
—	Protocol for the Accession of Yugoslavia to the General Agreement on Tariffs and Trade, 20 July 1966	GATT, Prot. Acc. Yugo.	—	Par. 1 (b)	Par. 4	Par. 2 (b)	Par. 9

Abbreviated agreement title used (1)	Agreement title (2)	Citation (3)	Qualification re application of pt. I (4)	Qualification re application of pt. II (5)	Different date re certain concessions (6)	Different date re certain parties (7)	Different termination period (8)
—	Protocol for the Accession of Korea to the General Agreement on Tariffs and Trade, 2 March 1967	GATT, Prot. Acc. Korea	—	Par. 1 (b)	Par. 4	Par. 2 (b)	Par. 9
—	Geneva (1967) Protocol to the General Agreement on Tariffs and Trade, 30 June 1967	GATT, Instrs. 1964-67 Conf., I, 21	—	—	Par. 4	—	—
—	Protocol for the Accession of Argentina to the General Agreement on Tariffs and Trade, 30 June 1967	GATT, Instrs. 1964-67 Conf., V, 3719	—	Par. 1 (b)	Par. 4	Par. 2 (b)	Par. 9
—	Protocol for the Accession of Iceland to the General Agreement on Tariffs and Trade, 30 June 1967	GATT, Instrs. 1964-67 Conf., V, 3763	—	Par. 1 (b)	Par. 4	Par. 2 (b)	Par. 9
—	Protocol for the Accession of Ireland to the General Agreement on Tariffs and Trade, 30 June 1967	GATT, Instrs. 1964-67 Conf., V, 3789	Par. 2 (b)	Par. 1 (b)	Par. 4	Par. 2 (c)	Par. 9
—	Protocol for the Accession of Poland to the General Agreement on Tariffs and Trade, 30 June 1967	GATT, Instrs. 1964-67 Conf., V, 3959	Pars. 4 and 7	Pars. 1 (b), 3, 4, 7, and 8	—	Par. 2 (b)	Par. 14

THE ATLANTIC COUNCIL
OF THE UNITED STATES

The Atlantic Council, established fourteen years ago, has as its prime goal to contribute to better relations among the countries of North America, Western Europe and Japan. These varied and complex relationships have been and will continue to be central to the major economic and political developments which affect our international integrity and domestic well-being.

In an increasingly interdependent world where "foreign" policy is ever more closely intertwined with "domestic" policies, there is a clear need for both official and private consideration of means of dealing with problems which transcend national frontiers. The Atlantic Council is a unique non-governmental, non-partisan, tax-exempt, educational, citizens' organization. It conducts its programs to promote better understanding of major international security, political and economic problems, foster informed public debate on these issues, and make substantive policy recommendations to both the administrative and legislative branches of the U.S. Government, as well as to the appropriate key international organizations.

ECONOMIC INTEGRATION AND THE LAW OF GATT
                    Pierre Lortie

THE GATT LEGAL SYSTEM AND WORLD TRADE DIPLOMACY
                    Robert E. Hudec

INTERNATIONAL FINANCIAL MARKETS: Development of the Present
System and Future Prospects*
                    Francis A. Lees and
                    Maximo Eng

FOREIGN TRADE AND U.S. POLICY
                    Leland B. Yeager and
                    David G. Tuerck

*Published for the Atlantic Council
of the United States*

THE FATE OF THE ATLANTIC COMMUNITY
                    Elliot R. Goodman

U.S. AGRICULTURE IN A WORLD CONTEXT: Policies and Approaches for
the Next Decade
                    edited by D. Gale Johnson
                    and John A. Schnittker

*Published for the Atlantic Institute for
International Affairs*

DEVELOPMENT WITHOUT DEPENDENCE*
                    Pierre Uri

DILEMMAS OF THE ATLANTIC ALLIANCE: Two Germanys, Scandinavia,
Canada, NATO and the EEC (Atlantic Institute Studies—I)
                    Peter Christian Ludz, H. Peter Dreyer,
                    Charles Pentland, and Lothar Ruhl

ENERGY, INFLATION, AND INTERNATIONAL ECONOMIC RELATIONS
(Atlantic Institute Studies—II)
                    Curt Gasteyger, Louis Camu,
                    and Jack N. Behrman

*Also available in paperback as PSS Student Editions